MY FATHER IS POLICE, LAH!

Colourful Memories of 1960s Colonial Singapore
Seen Through The Eyes of A Young Local Girl

ROWENA HAWKINS

My Father is Police, Lah!

By Rowena Hawkins

Trade Paper: 978-988-8904-31-0
Digital: 978-988-8904-30-3

© 2025 Rowena Hawkins

Biography & Autobiography

EB231

All rights reserved. No part of this book may be reproduced in material form, by any means, whether graphic, electronic, mechanical or other, including photocopying or information storage, in whole or in part. May not be used to prepare other publications without written permission from the publisher except in the case of brief quotations embodied in critical articles or reviews. For information contact info@earnshawbooks.com

Published in Hong Kong by Earnshaw Books Ltd.

Dedication

To my parents

Tez & Corrina

True stalwarts of Singapore

"Lah" is a typical Singapore-English ('Singlish') suffix USED for "added effect".
It has no specific meaning.

Contents

Prologue		ix
Chapter 1	A Bungalow and Personal Belongings	1
Chapter 2	Noblesse Oblige	19
Chapter 3	A Meeting at Magnolia	27
Chapter 4	Charity Really Begins at Home	37
Chapter 5	For the Love of Children	44
Chapter 6	Celebrations and Social Events	51
Chapter 7	Prince and Heir	62
Chapter 8	Horseplay	75
Chapter 9	Brush with the Supernatural	82
Chapter 10	Prophet's Consternation	90
Chapter 11	Extra-Curricular Activities	99
Chapter 12	House Guests	115
Chapter 13	Of Friendships Made and Pleasures Shared	130

Chapter 14	Grand Old Dame	144
Chapter 15	Honour Amongst Thieves	159
Chapter 16	Great Loss	174
Chapter 17	Chip off the Old Block	184
Chapter 18	Crossing the Equator	200
Chapter 19	Should Auld Acquaintance	213
Epilogue		224

Prologue

During the ancient Srivijayan Kingdom, a prince from Palembang discovered *Singapura* (Lion City) in 1299, several hundred years before Sir Stamford Raffles laid claim to the island in 1819. Sang Nila Utama, also known by his regnal title Sri Maharaja Sang Utama Parameswara Batara Sri Tri Buana (which can be translated as "Central Lord King of the Three Worlds"), would have been hard-pressed to imagine that his tiny island kingdom consisting of a handful of fishermen would 700 years later become a bustling metropolis, a melting pot of many races, creeds and religions. The 5.78 million residents of Singapore today consists of 75 percent ethnic Chinese, 12 percent Malays, 8 percent Indians, and the balance 5 percent of 'others', which I think is a far more congenial term than 'aliens' as seen at immigration counters in some airports around the world. When all is said and done, any Singaporean today is more than likely a descendant of an immigrant who left their place of origin and settled down on the island looking for greener pastures. And the grass was then, and still is, very green indeed. This is a City built inside a Garden.

It is a great tragedy that many youngsters who have been given responsible roles in companies and organisations, and the opportunity to succeed in a meritocratic nation, are unaware that the pioneer generation who made up the police, military, and administration personnel were all immigrants to Singapore. They fought for and built Singapore into the highly developed country it is today, so that these young people, their parents, their grandparents, and I daresay even their great-grandparents, are availed of the luxury of sleeping safely in their beds, worshipping in whatever religion they choose without fear of persecution, walking anywhere in Singapore without fear of criminal mischief, and certainly with no anarchy in the streets.

I remember wandering along the main street of Newbury, Berkshire, UK, a few years ago. I happened upon a stall set up by a British soldier attired in combat gear. It was nearing Remembrance Day, and the soldier was selling poppies and other memorabilia for the occasion. I bought some items and noticed that the embroidered name label on his tunic was also written in Arabic. I asked him whether he had fought in Iraq, and he replied that he had just returned from a posting in Afghanistan.

From the expression on his face, I gleaned that he must have had a really rough time there, and I hesitated to delve further. After leaving the stall, I went into a nearby shop and bought a coffee mug with a 'Smiley' icon on the front and back. I persuaded the shop staff to gift wrap the mug and took it to the soldier. I handed him the gift, and I said, "This is for you. Thank you for keeping England and the rest of the world safe."

His smile indicated he was really lost for words. "Fancy a gesture like this from a total stranger, and she is not even English," I imagined him thinking. His eyes looked straight into mine, he shook my hand and thanked me. I hope I made his day.

I am grateful to all those who have made sacrifices so that my parents and their children can live in a peaceful and safe world. Indeed, I always remember to thank commercial airline pilots before disembarking from flights for bringing me and the rest of the passengers safely to our destination. Ninety percent of passengers will not even make eye contact with the inflight crew, let alone the flight deck crew, if only to say 'thank you' for taking care of them during the flight.

After reading this, I hope you will remember all those, living or deceased, who have made countless sacrifices for the betterment of your own lives, those of your predecessors, your children, and of your country.

This biopic is a tribute to my immigrant parents, particularly my Dad,

ROWENA HAWKINS

and to all the other Pioneer Generation uniformed and civil government officers whose significant contributions and sacrifices have moulded Singapore into the safe, clean, religiously tolerant, law-abiding highly developed country it is today. May God Bless Them All!

Rowena Hawkins
Singapore
January 2025

1

A Bungalow and Personal Belongings

My mother, Corrina Gnai, had to have five servants to clean and maintain our colonial bungalow on a busy main road in downtown Singapore, at 409 New Bridge Road. All in all, our house was staffed to the hilt. It was a huge double-storey bungalow along the lines of seven similar ones stretched along the road, with at one end a traffic police station and at the other, the Sepoy Lines District Post Office. I did not know what a Sepoy was and why there had to be a line of them. These bungalows were allocated as housing perks to senior colonial government civil servants, and on our road, there were four senior police officers and four doctors, all immigrants of varied racial and religious cultures.

Ours was a corner bungalow, so we had the benefit of larger grounds than the other bungalows. Our huge garden was big enough to keep a pony, but we did not get one. My father was a 'champion of horses', serving as a horse racing steward for many years with the Singapore Turf Club, which is no more. My mother, however, feared that someone would be careless, fall off the pony, and die. As long as I can remember, my mother came up with some bizarre justification and figment of her colourful imagination about why a pony was a deadly idea. If we were to have followed her cautious thinking, it would have restricted development of a sense of adventure, even a normal lifestyle for the rest of us — me, Roweena Nurain nicknamed 'Girlie'; my older brother 'Azi', whose full name and titles are too long and numerous to list here, but will in a following Chapter; and my older sister Yuwari Sha'arifa who has a psychic gift and went her own way many years ago.

We would never have gotten out of bed if we had adhered to Mum's peculiar ideas. Our approach was to do something, whatever it was, first — then tell her later. Or not. This is something to which we all still subscribe to this day. She is now 97 years of age, at the time of writing this narrative and no one has yet died because of her bizarre fears, ideas and theories.

Notwithstanding the pony, or more to the point, the absence of one, I did, however, manage to lure several stray cats to settle down with us. Cats were a no-brainer for both my parents, so little persuasion was required to bring in these refugees. The cats were picked up from the monsoon drains surrounding our bungalow, and anything found wandering the streets was automatically decreed as mine. I expect these cats saw the invisible signpost which read, "All feline waifs and strays may enter here!" One bright spark amongst the servants' children suggested that if butter is spread on a cat's paw, it will entice the animal to stick around for better things to come. I found this rather perplexing as I was brought up to understand that butter was an accompaniment to toast and marmalade and was to be eaten. I could not imagine eating a buttered cat's paw.

The original cats propagated, and this is how we ended up with a colony of more than thirty-one cats at any given time, give or take one or two — through the turnover of feline life spans during the entire time we lived in that bungalow.

At one stage, Dad decided he would experiment with raising

quail. So he had a large wire cage constructed out of wire mesh and old bits of discarded wood, and in this he housed about a dozen quail. He had the cage placed on a sandpit outside our courtyard and kept them *al fresco*. Watching the cats taking a keen interest in the birds was most amusing. Some of the more ambitious felines sat precariously perched on the edge of a narrow windowsill or dangled from a branch of a sapling just a short distance from the cage and observed the movement of the quail. One could have imagined what went through their heads…so near yet so far. The cats sat for extended periods and looked intently at the quail without even a muscle twitching or a whisker flicking. So engrossed were they in their (hoped-for) tasty titbits that I often found this as an unspoken invitation to creep up behind the cat and let out a thunderous "Hoi!", whilst simultaneously smacking its rump for added effect, thereby sending the cat several feet in the air out of catastrophic (pun intended) fright.

On a couple of occasions, I watched one of the younger cat's eyes fixed on the cage for about five minutes. Not a whisker moved, its eyes did not even blink. Perhaps if a cat stares unblinking long enough at something in a cage, an optical illusion occurs whereby eventually, the cage wires will seem to disappear, and the cat's eyes will only see and focus on the objects inside the cage. If only I had a similar capacity for concentration in the classroom. Suddenly the cat sprang forward towards the cage only to get one tight smack to its face from the thick wire mesh, making the cat "Mee-yowl!" in shock rather than pain. Then it shot an intense imperious glance at me, hilariously laughing at its mishap, and then it walked away, alternately kicking its back legs from side to side with very precise syncopated movements and swishing its tail in regulated beats, indicating its indignation and undignified embarrassment.

MY FATHER IS POLICE, LAH!

The quail neither laid any eggs nor propagated during their entire lifespan under Dad's breeding project. Perhaps he had neglected to establish with the vendor the gender of each of the birds. Perhaps they were all the same gender. In any event, all the quail eventually perished, one by one, to Dad's utter disappointment. Perhaps he had also neglected to consider that keeping these fragile fowl out in the open subjected them to the harsh elements and made them more vulnerable to disease.

A typical colonial bungalow had the main house as the focal point with a gated driveway leading to a covered porch. At the back of the house was a long or short covered courtyard, depending on the size of the compound, leading to the servants' quarters and garage. The servants' quarters of our bungalow were self-sufficient, containing their own facilities: a kitchen, lavatories and bathrooms, and there were front verandahs facing the back fence and hedge of the compound. Next door to our bungalow was a private Methodist kindergarten linked to a Methodist Church, both of which used only Chinese. The Cantonese priest, whom we knew as Father Long, occupied the small vestry and lived there with his generously built Cantonese wife, who hailed from Hong Kong, his son and two daughters. My most vivid recollections of Mrs Long were that she was a fervent *kay poh*, a term for a busybody, of the highest order. Perceiving this in a positive vein, however, she came in handy as a walking encyclopaedia—always abreast of what was going on around the neighbourhood. Indeed, the whole of Singapore engaged in serious chatter in the Chinatown wet markets. The second most memorable aspect of Mrs Long's activities was creeping up to the edge of the lowest part of our hedge, surreptitiously peering from side to side and when she thought no one was looking— well, so she thought —and tipping her rubbish into our rubbish fireplace, a circle of boulders creating an open-plan incinerator.

On one occasion, I happened to be up in our guava tree, unbeknownst to Mrs Long. She came along with her rubbish basket and as usual crept to the edge of the low hedge, poised to tip the basket into our incinerator. At that moment, I swung off a thick guava branch like a chimpanzee and landed right in front of her and greeted her with a cheerful, "Good evening, Mrs Long!" just as she was about to hurl the basket's contents into our incinerator. My unexpected appearance, compounded by my sudden brisk outburst, gave the woman such an almighty fright that she tossed the basket in the air, and the airborne contents landed on her head.

Obviously, I was not going to hang around for the scolding.

The servants and their families had living quarters at the back of our bungalow. Saminah was in charge of the ground floor. Her husband Harris was our shop steward, as it were, and they had one daughter, Merina, who was my childhood playmate. Dad told me that Saminah and Harris, like Daeri and his wife Rukiah, were of Javanese origin. Rukiah was in charge of the upper floor, and her husband was our chauffeur Daeri, seconded by the Police Force. He graduated from the Police Training School and, after a couple of years as a police constable, was seconded to Dad as his batman and chauffeur. Therefore, it made perfect sense that he and Rukiah should move into our servants' quarters as they could save on their own living costs. They had no children, and so I became the daughter they never had.

Moona, who hailed from Minangkabau, was easily identifiable by her traditional headdress, which was a piece of cloth wound around the head like a turban, in such a manner that there were two pointed ends, like a pair of buffalo horns, sticking up at the top. Moona was the washer-woman. That was how Mum referred to her. This meant that she was in charge of the household laundry, which had to be done by hand using a wooden washboard, an oval-shaped large tin washtub, and bars of harsh laundry soap—the type that could also melt the fibres of fine fabrics. Washing machines had not been introduced, and the only effective dryer available was the sun. Plastic or rubber household gloves had not yet been invented, and this meant that poor Moona's hands and fingers were gnarled as her hands were constantly immersed in the harsh soapy water. She used copious amounts of starch, particularly needed for school uniforms and my father's tunic trousers. Then a bleach-like substance called *Blue* was added to the rinse. *Blue* was used to make clothes white. Go figure. Moona would also iron the starched apparel when dry, and it amused us no end to see my father's tunic trousers stand up by themselves after being ironed. Moona's husband was Zainal, and they had one daughter, Sabariah, who was also about my age.

Moona's method of washing clothes was to have the tin washtub filled with water whilst she scrubbed our clothes with soap on the washboard. This was fine except for one small detail— she kept the tap running into the tub like a continuous rinse cycle whilst the scrubbing process was underway, and this invariably lowered the rest of the household's water pressure. Woe betide you if you were taking a shower or, worse still, shampooing your hair. The moment Moona accessed flowing water, the rest of us did not. At once, there was usually heard from somewhere or other, whether the main house or the servant's quarters, a thunderous "*TUTUP PAIP!*" bellow in Malay, the order to turn off her laundry tap.

Zainal was, in effect, the sous chef, an apprentice to Zubaidah, our chief cook. Zubaidah, Dad reckoned, was a cross between a native Boyanese and a Banjarese—the former for her love of gold jewellery and the latter for her brave and authoritative behaviour. Zubaidah was the most striking among the team of servants. She was endearingly eccentric—actually delusional. Mum reckoned Zubaidah may have suffered a nervous breakdown when she had her first miscarriage, and the fact that later she was able to give birth to a normal child, Jaafar, seemed to offer little consolation. She often caked her face with thick white face powder made from crushed raw rice and lined her eyes with over-applied black liner, making her look like an Australian aboriginal at a tribal meeting. She wore odd footwear, and that did not necessarily mean two different shoes; one could be a shoe, and the other could be a slipper or she could go barefoot, and the variety and sequence changed frequently. She used to drag a small cardboard box on wheels around with her to the 'market' and return home with nothing in it. When I asked why the box in the cart was empty, she would lament that nobody at the 'market' wanted to sell her anything. Truth be told, she never ever got as far as the 'market'. She had simply imagined she had gone to the market. The farthest she ever ventured unaccompanied was to the end of the road where she sat on the roadside kerb, wrapped up some betel leaves, and chewed them. When satiated, she spat into the monsoon drain and then trudged back home dragging her empty box.

Sometimes, she returned with the box filled with old newspapers and empty tin cans, which she rummaged out of the neighbourhood dustbins. Her haul would then be accumulated in an empty wicker chicken coop kept at the back of the servants' quarters, which she guarded fiercely. These items were temporarily hoarded to be sold later to the *karangoni* man, the equivalent of a rag and bone man, for a few dollars. *Karangoni* was the local term in the Hakka dialect for a Chinese coolie rag and bone man. He wore a dark blue rough cotton Chinese tunic and baggy trousers, with a pointed wicker hat. He walked up and down our road shouting, "…goooni! Ka-raang-goooni!" He had prominent hollow cheeks, eyes bulging from sunken sockets and was painfully thin, indications of opium addiction. He pushed a makeshift metal trolley carrying a large gunny sack at one end and, at the other end a large wicker basket for empty bottles and tin cans. Discarded newspapers were weighed with a primitive set of *da-ching* scales, with a hook at one end of a metal rod and a bronze weight suspended at the other. Every time Zubaidah called out to the *karangoni* man, he pretended he did not hear her and endeavoured to shuffle past our gate unnoticed, with his head bowed, or pretended to wave at another peddler across the road in the hope that she would take that as a hint. But she was no pushover, despite being just five feet tall — "tall enough to grab an elephant by the balls," my mother often quipped.

Zubaidah had worked out how to accost the *karangoni* man and mastered it to a fine art. She would lie in wait, squatting behind the massive flame of the forest tree trunk at the front gate or some other hiding place near the gate, like a lioness waiting to pounce on a warthog. The coolie had no chance at all. This theatrical scene resembled a Laurel and Hardy comedy featuring one short fat dumpy Malay banshee tackling a painfully thin, ragged Chinese coolie with a pointed wicker hat. Just as the *karangoni* man thought that he had escaped her clutches, she would spring from her hiding place at a speed that belied her age, launching herself at the befuddled coolie and yelling an earth-shattering, "HOI APEK!"

Apek was the generic term used to address all Chinese peddlers and coolies. The sudden ear-splitting outburst was enough to awaken the dead, and perhaps the coolie often had near misses with heart attacks because of this woman. Zubaidah usually wore a baggy Straits Chinese-style *nyonya baju panjang*, which was the blouse of a two-piece traditional ensemble, and a black-and-white checked *sarong*, an Asian version of a long skirt usually sewn out of *batik* material. As such a sarong was usually worn by men, the garment probably belonged to her husband. Underneath her *baju panjang*, she had a thick, broad, green leather and woven cotton money belt that securely fastened the *sarong* wound around her waist. A *sarong* ordinarily caused some limitation to quick moves, but not to Zubaidah when it came to springing attacks on unsuspecting *karangoni* men or chasing someone around the kitchen with a cleaver for some misdemeanour or other. And, of course, don't forget the signature odd shoes. She had no difficulty bounding up to the hapless man, who predictably would stop dead in his tracks like a startled rabbit, and then dragged him and his trolley up our driveway, with the man in tow protesting furiously, "*Aiyaaah, mak cik, apasal? Lu orang semua gila kah!?*" The *karangoni man*, addressing her as *auntie* more out of fear than courtesy, was asking her what the matter was and if she had gone crazy.

Well, yes. She had. But only slightly.

There was an ongoing consternation every time these two did business. You see, Zubaidah knew the coolie was most adept at double-crossing customers. His bronze weight was not a one-kati weight but a five-kati weight. A kati, sometimes spelt 'catty', is a measure equivalent to roughly 1.3 pounds. Therefore, if she had twenty katis of newspapers to sell, he would attempt to pay her for four katis only because the scales would reach the balance point at four katis and not twenty, owing to the equilibrium weight assessed by a five-kati weight.

She heaved herself up to her fullest height, lunged at the coolie and smacked his wretched hat straight off his head with one swift blow. This assault was followed by a barrage of profanity that would have embarrassed a sailor. People tend to use profanity because they have a limited vocabulary, or are frustrated, or both. In Zubaidah's case, she was both. During the

MY FATHER IS POLICE, LAH!

entire sequence of Zubaidah's aerobic activity with the *karangoni* man, her *sarong* stayed put and not one hair on her perfectly coiffed bun fell out of place. Meanwhile, Merina, Sabariah, and I would be hiding nearby, well positioned to catch the *karangoni* man's flying hat as it was smacked off his head. Whoever caught the hat then ran off with it and wedged it on a high branch of the guava tree. The poor coolie then had to shimmy up and retrieve it, much to our amusement. Zubaidah was grateful to have three young agents upon whom she could rely to serve the coolie with a continuance of due retribution. She gave us a reward of a snack or treat from the kitchen afterwards.

I wondered whether the coolie had gotten used to this regular occurrence, or perhaps he was a glutton for punishment. He never modulated his tactics, or ever transacted an honest deal with Zubaidah. In fact, he actually began to see a bit of humour in it after a while. He chuckled and did a little dance waving his hands about and flashing a wide smile displaying a goldmine in his front teeth. Perhaps Zubaidah's eccentricity was contagious.

Zubaidah was quite the battle-axe in the kitchen as well — more so than my mother, who hesitated before confronting her for fear of having a basket of onions flung at poor Zainal, who often found himself in the line of fire. Zainal was in charge of culling and plucking the feathers off pre-slaughtered chickens, earlier purchased 'live' from the wet market, and performing other similar distasteful activities, which were too traumatising for my mother's psychologically fragile mind or beneath Zubaidah's station to execute herself.

Mum was the self-appointed minister of home affairs in our household, giving instructions and orders as to what was to be purchased, cooked, cleaned, retained, or discarded and by whom, but she made a point of steering clear of any duty or participation that involved the sight of blood.

And then there was 'Kebun' — not his real name, only because we were never formally introduced — but 'Kebun' means 'garden' in Malay. For all his sins, he was also Zubaidah's long-suffering husband. He was bestowed the task of single-handedly maintaining our huge garden and grounds, including but not restricted to looking after Dad's prized collection of orchids. The couple had one son, Jaafar, who helped his father with gardening after returning from school. Kebun had the misfortune to be completely bald. Dad, however, provided him with a suitable standard-issue *topi*; a spherical hard-topped helmet fashioned out of khaki canvas. The *topi* was particularly a must-have item for colonial planters working at rubber and oil palm plantations in Malaya. Kebun's *topi* was to protect his bald pate from the noonday sun, but Kebun often elected to go around without it — with disastrous results ranging from stray bird droppings deposited on his head to a projectile of saliva or worse still, the concoction from masticated betel leaves and saliva from some indiscriminate Tamil coolie, finding its resting place upon his head. These were routinely spat from the windows of stationary buses as he walked by.

Kebun was of particularly interest to me. He owned an Elswick bicycle, which I often borrowed, but Kebun had no idea he had lent it to facilitate my bicycle riding lessons. Both Merina and Sabariah were my learner wheel stabilisers, and therein lies the *modus operandi* of how I learnt to ride a bicycle, unbeknownst to Kebun or my mother, until the mission was accomplished.

Mum chose three young women to work as our *ayahs*. One of whom was Dad's youngest sister, Merifa, who was charged with tending to me; she pulled the short straw, as it were. Being of marriageable age, my parents brought Merifa to Singapore with hopes of engaging her to a Singapore-based 'spouse' of the same ethnicity as they, as was the case with my mother being matched with my father.

One of the other two nannies was a Chinese immigrant called *Ah Chwee*. It was unfortunate her name sounded like someone sneezing. She was charged with looking after my brother Azi. The third was charged with looking after my sickly older sister Yuwari.. She was a Thai immigrant whose real name now escapes me, not only because it was difficult to spell but also virtually impossible to pronounce. To make life easy for all, Mum called her Khun Nat. On account of Yuwari's sickly disposition as a child, Khun Nat surmised the reason for Yuwari's afflictions was of a supernatural nature; Yuwari could see 'ghosts' and this terrified her. Khun Nat persuaded Mum to let her take Yuwari to her home town in Surathani, which is a province in southern Thailand, to consult with a Buddhist monk renowned for tackling supernatural afflictions in children. My parents were extremely hesitant to accede to this suggestion, but Khun Nat assured them that this was the only way to overcome Yuwari's health troubles. Reluctantly my parents agreed and sent them both by train to Thailand. Mum sent monthly wages and maintenance fees to Khun Nat, who ultimately ended up undertaking the upbringing of her ward for the better part of thirteen years! I was only reunited with my elder sister twenty-five years later.

Mum paid each nanny a very good wage amounting to twenty Singapore Dollars a month. A gunny sack of rice weighing forty katis (approximately fifty-two pounds) at that time cost the princely sum of eighty cents. These ladies put their wages straight under their mattresses and, not having any overhead whatsoever, made an absolute fortune for themselves by the time we had outgrown the need for nannies. All of them were able to command handsome dowries, being women of formidable financial substance, in the playing field of marriage proposals.

However, Ah Chwee was a typical Chinese *black-and-white*

amah hailing from Guangdong Province and of the variety of Chinese women who belong to a sisterhood who undertake vows of celibacy. These Chinese women were easily identified by their pristine white Chinese tunic tops, *samfoos*, and their baggy black trousers. Their excessively long hair was typically plaited or else wound up and tied into a bun secured by a tortoise-shell hair clasp at the base of their neck. In Ah Chwee's case, however, she carefully centre-parted her long tresses, making sure the parting was perfectly centred, then plaited each side and wound each plait into a round bun on either side of her head. Each bun would then be secured with bobby pins, and the final flourish would be a tortoise-shell spiked adornment, not unlike the Malay-styled *cucuk sanggul*, a tortoise shell hair adornment sticking out of each bun like a pair of antennae. This invariably made her look like an extra-terrestrial being from planet Zogg, and worse still if she happened to cake her face with her requisite Chinese white pearl and rice face powder. Happening upon her, especially in the dead of night, could conceivably send someone into shock.

Women like Ah Chwee underwent a special hair-dressing ceremony to mark adulthood and the renouncement of marriage. They worshipped the goddess *Kwan Yin*, the Goddess of Mercy, who they regarded as the matron saint of their sisterhood. Mum regarded Ah Chwee as an exceptional *ayah or amah*, the latter being the Cantonese equivalent. She was painstakingly punctual when feeding her charge, always scrupulously neat in appearance and had a wonderful singing voice, which could even get a hard-core coffee addict to fall asleep on command. Her unusually ample bosom fixed upon her rotund person provided a comfortable headrest for my brother while she lulled him to sleep. She was partial to consuming large quantities of chicken feet and chicken necks, the latter reputedly infused with various amounts of chicken *artificial enhancers*. She was about the same size as the indomitable Zubaidah, but whereas Zubaidah was short and stout, Ah Chwee was short and rotund; if one were able to push her limbs and head into her torso, one could probably bounce her around like a beach ball. Some days Ah Chwee made a special trip to the market to purchase vegetables, some fruit offerings, and other religious items for the *Kwan Yin* Deity she displayed on her little altar. But she never left her ward behind. So, when Azi was young, she bundled him up in a *batik sarong* sling — a commonly used apparatus favoured by ethnic Malay and Chinese women and draped diagonally across their torsos. *Ayahs* often used them as a hands-free baby or child carriage. Ah Chwee draped the sling containing Azi from her shoulder diagonally across her torso between her breasts. As she was so short, Azi would have his legs straddling her waist, with his feet almost touching the ground as she waddled along. As he grew older, he walked alongside her with Ah Chwee holding tightly onto his hand as she went on her market jaunts.

The market was walking distance from the house, but there were times when Ah Chwee was late in returning after her shopping. When asked to explain her tardiness, she would lament in a voice ten decibels too loud, "*Aiyaah Missee-ah, becha 'tak mau angkat laaah. Becha cakap balang belat, olang pun belat, dia 'tak mahu angkat laaah*" in Malay doused with a heavy Cantonese accent. This amusing explanation, that the trishaw coolie did not want to accept her as a fare because he observed that she looked like a very heavy person to transport and the contents of her shopping baskets also appeared to match her in weight and size, amused my mother more than infuriated her.

I remember one particular occasion, Ah Chwee went to a temple in nearby Chinatown to offer fruits to Kwan Yin on the festive occasion of her 'birthday'. Chinatown was not far from where we lived; about two or three bus stops away and the whole expedition should have taken not more than an hour. However, after four hours, Ah Chwee had still not returned, and this set off the alarm bells amongst the other servants. Mercifully, she had not taken Azi with her that day as this would have sent my mother immediately into hysteria mode. It would not need to take a four-hour delay to push Mum off the rails; thirty minutes beyond the prescribed timeframe would have sufficed for her to command Dad to raise a police search party for her son missing in action.

Ah Chwee finally arrived home five hours later, safe but visibly flustered and somewhat bedraggled without any visible injuries. But her desperate attempt to smooth the numerous wisps of loose and dishevelled hair that had broken loose from her normally perfect coiffure lent an appearance of someone who had just hiked up Bukit Timah Hill in record time. She explained that whilst taking the bus home, she entered into a 'staring' match with a salacious Bengali or Sikh passenger, who took a keen interest in her ample bosom. As she was attired in her best *samfoo* tailored to accentuate her upper torso, this drew unwanted attention from the *Sikh,* who invariably looked fixedly at her upper body, alternating his gaze between her bosom and her face. A Chinese woman with large breasts was uncommon in those days. So Ah Chwee glared back menacingly at him, slowly bringing her large Chinese heavily waxed paper umbrella into sight as a warning gesture.

"*Apasal Nonya, 'lu mahu gado saya, ah?*" the Sikh taunted in Malay, challenging Ah Chwee to enter into a fight with him.

"*Lu 'Mangkali olang' gila 'pelempuan' ah? Ta'la tengok pelempuan dulu kah?*" she snorted back at him, returning his taunts in her signature Cantonese-accentuated Malay, alleging that all Bengali men are woman-crazy, and asking this particular fellow if he had never seen a woman before. What Ah Chwee lacked in height, she made up for with strong vocal cords. This created some tension between the Bengali, Ah Chwee, the bus conductor, and a few other passengers who rose to Ah Chwee's defence. But the incident distracted Ah Chwee so that she had missed her bus stop and they were now on their way to Bukit Timah Road, the trunk road leading to the Johore Causeway linking Peninsular Malaya to Singapore. She then had to get off at the next bus stop, which was ten miles from home, to catch another bus home.

Throughout the entire period of Ah Chwee's service to my mum, there was only one occasion when she fell short of Mum's high expectations; she inadvertently dropped my brother on his head when lifting him out of his high chair. That perhaps accounts for my brother turning out the way he did! Miraculously, he suffered no serious injury, except that the shock of falling over gave him a slight fever, which caused Mum to fly into panic mode, enough to consider terminating Ah Chwee's services forthwith. But Azi had fallen only a short distance as she was lowering him to the floor and it actually did not cause him any serious damage. Immediately after his fall, Ah Chwee prepared a most efficacious herbal poultice, which she applied to his forehead. The poultice brought the fever down, and the lump and dent to his head later subsided. This appeased my panic-stricken mum sufficiently into re-considering Ah Chwee's dismissal, but I have always attributed the chestnut shape of Azi's head to that fall. Mum disagreed, saying she had had an insatiable craving for chestnuts the night before Azi was born and consumed a hefty amount of them; hence, he was born with a chestnut-shaped head.

Most of our domestic staff was Malay, except for Ah Chwee and Khun Nat. Oh, and did I mention that not one of the female Malay domestic staff wore the *hijab* in those days, despite being Muslims? In the early 1960s, Malay women simply draped over their heads a short *sarong or kain sarong,* as it was sometimes called, holding it over their heads with both hands like a short 'tent'. When going outdoors, this was primarily to shelter their heads from the tropical sun. Alternatively, a shawl made of flimsy delicate material known as a *selendang* was draped casually over the head and shoulders or hung loosely upon one shoulder when not used to shield the wearer from the sun. The *selendang* eventually took over from the *kain* s*arong* as the latter was rather cumbersome and made the women look like Franciscan friars.

Commendably, Mum elected not to be a stay-at-home housewife. Being an intelligent and accomplished lady, in addition to being the eldest daughter of a District Officer, she decided to apply for a position in Government and became an Assistant Director of the Counselling and Advice Section in the Ministry of Social Affairs, a position she held for a quarter of a century. In those days, women of distinguished parentage were not encouraged to hold any kind of job, but she was an ace at breaking down barriers to achieve her own designs, even though she fervently forbid the same of her siblings and children. My father was not going to begin to try to dissuade her. Discretion being the better part of the valour adage was in full force.

My parents, therefore, were among the precious few Asians in colonial Singapore who fell under the category of *Double Income* parents. This, coupled with their respective lineage, gave us the advantage of being a privileged family. My parents also paid for the servants' children's education. Both Merina and Sabariah went to local government schools, as did Jaafar, whereas I was sent to an elite Methodist school for girls. Daeri, our chauffeur, ferried the servants' children to and from their schools early in the morning before returning to take my parents to their offices. So really, even the servants' children had a fairly comfortable lifestyle, courtesy of my Dad's goodness.

MY FATHER IS POLICE, LAH!

Maintaining such a lifestyle inevitably resulted in high overheads for my parents. But life was good then. You could buy a hot meal for ten cents and get change.

2

NOBLESSE OBLIGE

My father, Tuanku Sabir Zainabdul, was a Malay prince, a direct descendant of a royal family exiled to Ceylon (now Sri Lanka) during the Dutch colonisation of Batawie, which was the local name for Dutch Batavia. The title within his *actual* given name attests to his lineage, 'Tuanku'. 'Tuanku' 'Tuan' or in some other Malay versions, 'Tengku', stands for 'prince' or 'princess'. But to his British friends, my Dad was 'Tez'. I do not know when and how my father earned the name "Tez" as I was not born yet. However, I can only surmise it is an anglicised half-hearted acronym chosen by his British peers to simplify his full name. He was awarded several accolades throughout his military and police career and by the time he passed away in 2014, his credentials included, PPA, PBS, BBM and BBM. He was a dedicated Freemason, and the Worshipful Master of his mother lodge, Lodge Singapore 7178 E.C.

The Dutch colonials offered two options to the royal families of the East Indies Archipelago sultanates; submit, pay homage and become servile to their new masters, or be exiled. This would invariably mean having all entitlements, palaces, and chattels forfeited, and to add insult to injury, they had to pay a levy to the colonial masters. Some royal families were exiled to Cape Town,

South Africa, which led to the emergence of the Cape Malays. Others landed in the Malay Peninsula, installing themselves as rulers within their own communities and creating their own sultanates. Dad's ancestors refused to yield and were exiled together with members of the royal court and their retinues to Ceylon, with the penalty of forfeiting all their material wealth and being stripped of their regnal titles, heritage, and realm, whilst taking the long and arduous journey to their country of exile with hardly any money, food or supplies to sustain them. Those who survived the journey and reached Ceylon combined their families into one large community, thereby establishing the Ceylon Malay community.

Dad's natural mother died when he was fifteen. His father remarried her sister, as was the normal practice amongst the Ceylon Malay royal families to keep the lineage intact and pure. In those ancient times, there were no genetics specialists around to tell them about the complications of inbreeding, although from somewhere around my paternal grandfather's time, I traced some clandestine 'unofficial' inter-marriages, involving unions with the local Singhalese women, British, Dutch, and even Chinese immigrants in Ceylon.

Dad enlisted in the British Army garrison stationed in Ceylon, which was at that time still a British colony. This turned out to be the game changer in his life. He was from a privileged family and received his education at a British school, not a local Singhalese medium school. From there, he progressed to the British Military College before being posted to Singapore to join the British Forces stationed there. And that is how he came to be in Singapore as a young, handsome bachelor.

Too much economic success, and in Dad's case, also social success, should not make one cavalier. Dad was a very patient gentleman. 'Patience' is reflected in one of his official given names which is a derivative of the Arabic word '*Sabur*'. I expect this largely contributed to his being able to put up with my Mum for more than sixty years. In fact, I'm pretty sure it did; I often heard him mumble under his breath shortly after Mum walked away from him in a huff. "My name means patience..." But this does not in the least indicate that Dad was a pushover.

"A Superior man is modest in his speech but excels in his actions," said Confucius, and Dad fitted the bill to a tee.

Shortly after, the British Forces in Singapore seconded him to the Police Force where he trained as a Detective Inspector. His was in the brigade of police officers who received their training through real police pursuits and ventures, such as, for example, hiding in ditches to pounce on criminals and members of triads in Singapore. His training was not of the paper pusher variety, turning out those who are immediately conferred officer's rank after graduating from university. There were also instances when he and other detective trainees were ordered to hide in the local cemetery, lying upon graves, armed with batons or revolvers and camouflaging themselves under their thick black rubber police standard-issue raincoats to arrest grave robbers. I thought the need for revolvers was a tad superfluous — after all, any robber seeing a dark shape in the thick of the night in a cemetery suddenly emerging from a grave would not need to be asked twice to stick around and put up a fight, now, would they?

I was Dad's 'shadow' wherever and whenever possible. This meant I was also a regular feature at the Police Officers' Mess where Dad would retreat after a day of active field duty or during the weekends, to enjoy a few 'stingers' with the other detectives. This Anglicised word 'stinger' was coined from the Malay word 'sa-tengah', meaning a half-shot of whiskey. It was the colonial norm: a traditional old-guard courtesy to offer a guest. "Would you care to have the other half?" as an invitation to have the other 'half shot' of whiskey—and simultaneously, an indication that the guest should down it and exit after *one for the road*.

Children were meant to be seen and not heard in those days, particularly so in a Police Officers' Mess. I would sit quietly in a chair at what they thought was a safe distance and listen to my Dad and his fellow officers regale listeners with tales of what they got up to during fieldwork. My capacity to hear a whisper at ten paces was formidable. Not all of it was police work; many of the detectives were still single and living in unmarried officers' quarters. So, the pursuit of extra-curricular activities ran rampant among the bachelors, who often ended up in shotgun marriages. Apparently, Dad had no shortage of female company: he was a good-looking, slim gentleman and cut a distinguished figure, especially in his formal Mess Kit. There is no shortage of women who go weak in the knees at the sight of an officer in uniform. Dad was a well-mannered, well-spoken officer, fluent in his command of the English language and, more importantly, a gentleman even at the most difficult of times. On account of the latter, there are some things that an officer and gentleman are not at liberty to divulge openly and to this end, I will be somewhat discreet.

A few years after the end of World War II, he received a telegram from his father instructing him to return home immediately to Ceylon, as marriage was being arranged for him. Dad had no intention of getting married at that time, as he was still enjoying the freedom and pleasures of bachelorhood. Little did he know then that one of the biggest merits of not getting married was that he would not have had to put up with my mother for the next sixty years. He sent a reply to his father saying that he was not able to get permission and leave from his Commanding Officer to return home to get married.

This was a big fat lie—but desperate times call for desperate measures. Short of telling my grandfather he was quite content with his Eurasian de-facto wife and would be getting engaged and marrying her shortly, with or without my grandfather's knowledge, Dad could not think of a more plausible excuse. But happily this relationship did not lead to marriage, as otherwise someone else would be narrating this story.

My grandfather then wrote, "Leave the Police Force and come back to get married, otherwise, it will not be good for you." The last phrase did not mean my Dad stood the prospect of indigestion as a penalty. His father was the Community Chieftain, the equivalent of being the Sultan amongst the Ceylon Malay Community. Correspondingly, this made Dad 'Crown Prince and Heir'. If Dad was to do anything to disgrace the Ruler -- and being disobedient about an arranged marriage would fall into this category -- the 'elders' would conveniently arrange for an *accident* to befall Dad, designed to remove him from our planet for eternity.

Thus, under threat of disgrace, premature demise, or both, Dad had no option but to seek permission from his Commanding Officer for home leave, promising to return to Singapore with a wife. Permission having been granted, much to his disappointment, my father took a slow boat home—a very, very, slow boat. He might have even thought to paddle the vessel himself to buy time. In keeping with the chivalrous standards with which he was reared and groomed, he gently broke the news to his distraught Eurasian de-facto wife, introduced her to a fellow police officer, and left her with provisions, financially and otherwise, before he left to meet his 'arranged' bride. His former Eurasian partner eventually married the other officer, and they raised their own family. They left Singapore soon after marriage to settle in the United Kingdom. Later, upon bringing his wife to Singapore, my father was careful to ensure that *ne'er the 'twain shall meet.*

MY FATHER IS POLICE, LAH!

Many years later, Dad vividly related the epic adventure of his marriage. Mum picked out the better parts, which lauded her personally and conveniently denied everything else as a fabrication of his colourful imagination.

It took him the better part of four weeks to reach his destination by ship. Upon arrival, he was immediately ushered to the bride's house where for the first time, he cast eyes on his future bride, my mother, who had reached the age of 28. He was thereupon permitted, together with a squadron of five servants and two soon-to-be sisters-in-law acting as chaperones, to accompany his soon-to-be wife to the local wet market to purchase comestibles. Some saw this as an opportunity to ignite romance between the two of them — who knows, perhaps even to ignite the *sacred flame* between a man and a woman. But hazarding a guess and more to the point, the aim was also to establish whether Dad had the financial capacity to pay for Mum's upkeep.

I suppose in those days, the elders did not understand that romance neither can be sought nor forced upon anyone — and certainly not through shopping in a smelly wet market, with goats, cattle, and chicken in coops for sale, and other peddlers boisterously advertising their wares.

My mother's relatively advanced age as a female candidate for a marriage proposal presented a huge conundrum for her side of the family, as girls were expected to be wives and mothers before they reached the age of 21. In some instances, girls were married off as soon as they reached puberty. Mum was the eldest daughter of eleven children: nine girls and two boys. As was the custom then, none of the other girls could marry before the eldest girl. She apparently was a renegade in her day and age; she secretly did many things that girls of noble lineage were stringently forbidden to do, on the premise that working girls or young women, or indeed, young girls outside of the safety of their homes, were deemed to be members of the subservient lower classes.

She took ballet lessons, paying for them with her own money, which she earned as a schoolteacher. With there being the scarcity of ballet shoes available then, let alone *pointe* ballet shoes; she had the capacity to strike an adage pose on tiptoes, without wearing proper *pointe* ballet shoes. I expect the ballet school she attended must have been run by the *Mems* of British Colonial Officers stationed in Ceylon and as Mum was educated in English and was a schoolteacher no less, she must have coerced these women into allowing her to join their ballet classes. She was a striking beauty and used her poise and beauty to be professionally photographed for a fee. A handsome fee, actually. I expect that at some stage in her career, she must have been earning more money than her father, a District Officer, who was serving under the Ceylon Colonial Governor.

She secretly took piano lessons in the school where she taught; I should mention here that my grandfather had no idea whatsoever that my mother was up to all sorts of high jinks whilst he was dutifully at his workplace and assuming all was in order at home. She would simply be back home before my grandfather returned from work and conducted the *roll call* of his daughters! Once or twice, my mum would be inadvertently delayed returning on time, and my grandfather would go into a frenzy looking for his eldest daughter. But she was also, secretly, his favourite daughter.

I expect Mum's great beauty, poise, and elegance must have swung Dad right out of his leather army boots. She is an educated lady with a remarkable command of English for a non-British woman of that day and age anyway, and well-versed in music, making her a highly attractive marriage prospect. The marriage date was set, and the next time they met, it was on their wedding *pelamin,* an elaborately decorated dais or platform. Dad had to pay the customary dowry to an elder from Mum's family, and this cost him the princely sum of 100 Ceylon Rupees which in those days, could feed a village for a month. Mum's *take* on this was, "I don't come cheap!"

Today, 100 Rupees would buy one coconut in Sri Lanka.

The wedding ceremony took the better part of four days. At the end of it all, Mum had already packed up her trousseau into four large steel trunks, the type that the Sicilian mafia use to dispose of their victims, and these accompanied my parents on their long voyage back to what was to become her new home, Singapore.

Mum was very evidently her father's favourite daughter, and her marrying and leaving the family home was to her father like losing the sunshine of his life. It was unbearable. Every father hurts when they lose a daughter to marriage; to my grandfather, the bruising was even more painful, more like a wound, and, in fact, tragic. Three days after my parents arrived in Singapore, Mum received a telegram from Ceylon. Her father had unexpectedly passed away. She grieved and cried alone. She was in a strange place where she had no friends, siblings, relatives, and a husband who could not be with her much to console and empathise. He had to go to work.

At this precise time, she cursed being married, cursed being in Singapore, and even cursed her very existence. Dad was occupied with his military duties, and he could not quite tell his Commanding Officer, "Excuse me, Sir, I need time off because my wife is sad and alone at home." Especially as he had just returned to Singapore after taking an extended home leave to get married. It took her a long time to recuperate from this tragedy.

But Mum's resoluteness and dignity won through. She was and still is that kind of woman, best described as stoic.

3

Meeting at Magnolia Milk Bar

Dad was a regular at the Magnolia Milk Bar. I was only a secondary reason that contributed to his regular appearances there. The main reason was that he had a network of informers amongst the staff. The establishment was situated on the legendary Orchard Road, which was and still is the main 'happening' street in downtown Singapore. Beside it was the Cold Storage Supermarket, which catered to the expatriate community of housewives as the company imported all sorts of British and European-made foodstuffs and was probably the main supplier of imported meat, poultry, seafood, and frozen produce.

The waitresses all knew him and addressed him as 'Boss'. He was not the owner of the Milk Bar—the Cold Storage Supermarket Company owned it—but as he often came in wearing his police uniform, I surmise this was largely the reason for his being awarded that title. There was no need for an order to be placed; it was the same every time.

"One chicken pie, a packet of Magnolia fresh milk for the 'girl' and a pot of Ceylon tea for me, please," Dad would request.

Daeri would be sent off with a few coins to get his own *teh tarik* from a nearby tea hawker while waiting for us. *Teh Tarik* literally means 'pulled tea' in Malay—so called because of the action of the vendor pouring prepared milk tea from one enamel container into another using long upward movements of his arms as in a pulling or stretching action, in alternate sequence.

Our order arrived, and the chicken pie, as always, looked inviting and appetising—except that as children of a privileged family, we were not allowed to tuck in enthusiastically, as per Mum's etiquette orders, until she, or in this case, Dad, gave us permission to begin eating. I could feel the juices in my mouth building up almost to a froth and I had to swallow hard not to let a dribble of saliva escape. The waitress smiled at me, seemingly amazed yet once more, at the level of discipline I possessed in not making a grab for the refreshments, as might less disciplined children. She turned to Dad and quipped, "Waah, Boss, your daughter so big now, *aah (a commonly used Singaporean English or 'Singlish' expression)* to extend a carefully contemplated degree of congeniality with Dad.

"Big? She's still eight. You only saw her last month. Has she grown so fast since then?" my Dad replied in a jocular tone, so as not to offend the waitress in case the next time around, she should spit into his tea out of bruised feelings and malice.

The waitress giggled coyly and invited us to enjoy our refreshments, leaving the bill in a tray in front of my Dad. He always left a generous tip for the serving staff, knowing full well these blue-collar workers may have direct or indirect connections with the criminal underworld and could generally be relied upon for a tip-off, if and when the need arose.

Detective Inspector Peter Butterworth, and his daughter Patricia, who was my age, entered the Milk Bar. Mr Butterworth, as I was taught to address him, approached us upon seeing us seated there. He gave an obligatory salute to Dad who was then his Superior Officer, and then formalities having been duly executed and concluded, amicably greeted us.

"I say, Tez!" he called out to Dad.

"I say, Peter!" was Dad's automated and hearty response. I used to wonder a lot about this British form of salutation, "I say!" Everyone starts off with an 'I say,' but then they don't say anything afterwards.

I had a girlie crush on Mr Butterworth. The very prospect of seeing him in person immediately distracted my attention from the chicken pie. The pie was no match for what had approached our table; the pie would be gone in sixty seconds, but Mr Butterworth would be around for quite a bit longer for me to hopelessly ogle him.

"Take a seat, why don't you..." Dad invited in a half-satirical tone. I looked carefully at Dad, wondering where he wanted Mr Butterworth to take the seat. As they sat down with us at our table, the proverbial 'penny' finally dropped, thereupon shedding much-needed light on what Dad's comment meant.

I was quite an impressionable child, I must say.

As they sat down at our table, Mr Butterworth ruffled my hair and said jovially. "Hello, Girlie! Where have you been today? Been a good girl?" he enquired perfunctorily, not really wanting to know the answers. His focus was actually on Dad and not me, and in any case, children were meant to be seen, and not heard.

Mr Butterworth was a tall, slim man with distinctive blue eyes and equally striking blonde tousled hair shorn short, complying with police regulations. He had finely chiselled features in a handsomely defined face, and his biceps were straining against his khaki tunic sleeve in an effort to be released from their containment as he first saluted Dad, and then shook his hand. In today's times, I expect I could have easily drooled over and brazenly flirted with a man possessing this level of attractiveness; sadly, I was born about twenty-five years too late.

Patricia or 'Patty' as we knew her, and I were ballet chums.

MY FATHER IS POLICE, LAH!

We were enrolled in the same ballet school, the Red Shoes School of Ballet on Orange Grove Road—an establishment that also served as a private kindergarten on weekdays for children from noble families. It was a stately double-storey colonial bungalow built on raised ground in a quiet prime residential district. The distinctive feature I remember was the line of Travellers' Palm trees at the front façade, abutting the bungalow's picket fence. In earlier years the district must have been used for the cultivation of oranges, hence, the road's name.

Patty and I were in the same Saturday ballet class and had progressed to Grade 3. By the time we were eight years old, we had undergone two formal Royal School of Ballet Examinations and had achieved certification. After ballet class, it was a trip down to the Magnolia Milk Bar to replace the energy loss from ballet dancing. We also attended each other's birthday parties, which were always held on a grand scale as both families lived in double-storey colonial bungalows, albeit in different districts, and led very privileged lives.

"What would you like to have, Patty?" Mr Butterworth interjected in our children's chatter.

"A curry puff and an F & N Orange, please, Daddy. May I have lots of ice with my orange drink, please, Daddy?" Patty asked politely, a far cry from the terminology and tone often heard from modern-day 'princes' and 'princesses'—"I WANT Coke! I WANT ice! NOW!" This sort of arrogance from the young local kids of today leads one to think that these children are misled, by their own parents no less, into believing they are superior and self-assured to the point of being regarded as demi-gods, when in fact, their behaviour is often downright spoilt and rude. Such children gain attention by losing respect. Most parents today will feel guilty when something goes wrong with their kids, but at the same time, elect for denial in attitude.

Heavily iced drinks were more a necessity than a luxury amongst the heat-addled British living in the tropics, as particularly young children and their *Mems*, the title given to British colonial wives, found it exhaustingly difficult to cope with the tropical heat. Before the onset of global warming and its devastating consequences, the temperature brought on by the noonday sun in the 1960s hardly rose above 25°C. Air-conditioned room temperatures today, however, are set to this very same temperature level in government offices and the same is recommended for private offices, within an environment where the current mean daily temperatures reach 33 to 38 degrees Celsius.

After giving their refreshments order to the same waitress, who was quick to recognise Mr Butterworth and came forward, beaming at him with a thirty-two-toothed smile, went away with his order, looking somewhat dejected that Mr Butterworth had not bothered to give her a second look. I guess she had long admired his good looks as would have scores of other young girls and recognised his potential value as an *ang moh* (a Hokkien expression to describe a Caucasian. The literal translation is 'red hair') boyfriend-cum-sugar daddy. Mr Butterworth then turned and looked in the direction of my father and said quietly but in a serious tone, "Tez, something's amiss in the Muslim Quarter. With the birthday of Prophet Muhammed's PBUH *('Peace Be Upon Him'. A suffix recited/written after a mention of the Prophet Mohammed's (PBUH) name as a means of offering respect to him by Muslims), and as a courtesy to Muslims, by non-Muslims)* birthday approaching, there is talk of racial riots erupting with the Chinese."

I remember Dad straightening himself in his chair and looking intently at Mr Butterworth.

"What does the OC think is going to happen?" Dad asked. 'OC' is police jargon for the Officer-in-Charge of a Divisional Police Station. Both Dad and Mr Butterworth were then attached to the Orchard Road Division Station.

"THAT came from the OC," Mr Butterworth hissed through his gritted straight white teeth. "Doesn't look good. OC is preparing to leave with his family and is heading outstation to Malaya over the next few days. Can you believe this?"

My father simmered angrily. He never displayed outbursts of temper at home, either. I guess he would not dare with Mum around, whereupon even if he felt the urge to bellow something at her overbearing autocratic style, he also knew when discretion was the better part of valour. But he was quite different in the company of constables, junior officers, and, for sure, when interrogating criminal suspects. But I always knew that it would be prudent to observe my own silence whenever I noticed his eyebrows meet each other in the middle of his forehead. And on this occasion, his eyebrows did meet in the middle. I might not have, but Dad certainly knew what was to come in the not-so-far distant future.

"OC is skipping town, with the prospect of imminent racial riots?" my Dad repeated, in utter disbelief.

"Rumour has it that CP may also go with him to their bungalows in Penang," added Mr Butterworth. CP was 'police speak' for the Commissioner of Police. This last revelation forced my father to purse his lips.

"I see," he said in a solemn tone; the same tone he used each time I attempted to give him some hapless, totally implausible excuse as to why I had yet another not-so-brilliant school report card. "Why, are there, all these grades, in red ink, Girl?" he would ask, slowly articulating each word carefully and in a monotone. "Daaad, I think... maybe... could be... the teacher ran out of blue ink?" would be my hopeless but creative response. What made matters worse was the class teacher's recurring written remarks virtually every term: "Capable of better work. Tends to be talkative and playful in class."

"So, who is expected to be acting OC during their absence?" Dad asked.

"You, Tez. You are the most senior officer below the rank of OC," Mr Butterworth replied in a matter-of-fact tone. Dad almost choked on his tea. It wasn't not very often, but there were times when my father became speechless, an attribute that would better suit my mother. This was one such time.

"Right you are," he said as an observation, when he finally recovered from the shock.

"Why haven't you been selected to lead the riot squads? You are closer to being a colonial officer than I," Dad said, hoping to unload this unwanted and obviously dangerous responsibility on Mr Butterworth.

"Probably because I have nothing to do with Intelligence," Mr Butterworth replied, not realising his remark left himself vulnerable to a bit of Dad's wicked wit.

"That is obvious to all of us!" Dad quipped with a wide grin displaying his signature winsome smile. Dad possessed a natural sense of humour and often came up with an amusing anecdote or punchline, which contributed to his popularity at the Senior Police Officers' Mess. Both officers started laughing, raising a toast to one another with their cups of tea.

"'Scuse Boss, jus' now aah, boss…Atchully' I don' wan' listen you and Mister Peter talking aah, you know lah…but I listen *one aah*," (a common Singlish suffix used for emphasis) came the soto voce words from behind our cubicle. Dad turned around and Mr Butterworth looked up, both of them regarding the face of none other than our enterprising waitress, who had been clearing, or

MY FATHER IS POLICE, LAH!

pretending to clear the table in the cubicle behind us, and had now emerged to reveal her presence.

"Only because you wanted to listen!" quipped Mr Butterworth, which even caused Patty and me to giggle.

We knew her as 'Nancy'; that was the name printed on her identity badge, anyway. Nancy bent forward to face the two police officers and said in a hushed tone, "Boss-ah, Mister Peter-ah, I listen, my boyfriend, talk yesterday *one aah* ... his gang go make trouble with Malay peoples on Muslim holiday day *wor* (a Singlish expression commonly used as a suffix for emphasis).

"Start near to Padang. You don' say I say you, *aah*," she hissed. "Wait after my boyfriend," and then she ended the sentence with a gesture of her hand mimicking a slicing action across her throat.

Then she quickly stood upright and pretended to ask, if we wanted to order anything else, knowing full well that both our orders were quite complete.

The Padang, to which Nancy referred, is a large quadrangle grass field in front of the steps of the Singapore City Hall in the Chambers of which, Admiral Lord Louis Mountbatten received the Surrender Instrument from General Seishiro Itagaki on September 12, 1945, at the end of the Japanese Occupation of Singapore.

Both Dad and Mr Butterworth placed a $5 tip each on the tray, and Nancy quickly snatched away the money and stuffed it inside her waitress tunic's bodice before the supervisor could catch sight of the two notes. In the 1960s, $10 would have been the equivalent of $100 today, and that would buy a lot of pretty fancy dresses at the *pasar malam*, a weekly night market for all manner of clothing, haberdashery, cooked food, produce, and comestibles sold at make-shift hawker stalls. Nancy could well be the next 'queen' of the Beauty World Cabaret hostesses, a job which she undertook at night, after her waitressing job at the

Magnolia Milk Bar. What an antithesis of occupational scenarios!

After we had finished our refreshments, Dad and Mr Butterworth stood up to leave. It was good timing for us to exit the Milk Bar, saying our goodbyes to Nancy. Daeri had just brought the car to the front entrance, where a small group of street urchins had congregated, their faces pressed against the glass panels, making them look amusingly grotesque. As we stepped outside, Dad reached into his uniform trouser pocket and pulled out his small black leather coin purse. He then proceeded to take one coin out at a time and press each coin into every child's outstretched hand. As he was in uniform, the children knew to be on B.B. (best behaviour) and did not attempt to turn rowdy and make a grab for his coin purse. They just beamed with delight at receiving the means to purchase an ice cream popsicle. One might think this would be a regular occurrence and each subsequent occasion increasing the number of recipients of Dad's generosity. This could have been so, if not for the propinquity of a burly giant of a Sikh watchman, known as a *jaga*, a Malay word used both as a noun and verb meaning *guard*, employed by the Cold Storage Company. His role included regularly patrolling the vicinity to ward off undesirable onlookers, street urchins and beggars.

"Any chance of a ride to the Beach Road Station, Tez?" asked Mr Butterworth as we were about to get into Dad's Austin.

"You're quite out of the way from where we're going, Peter," Dad replied.

"Not if you drive us there," chuckled Peter, flashing a wide smile of his perfect brilliant white teeth. And so we set off to first leave Mr Butterworth and Patty at the Beach Road Police Station. As we entered the gates of the Station, the two sentry policemen on each side of the gate sprang to stand rigidly to attention and saluted both officers. Patty and I, who were seated on opposite window sides, with Mr Butterworth wedged between us like a 'piggy-in-the-middle', were ever ready to emulate our fathers' police officers' etiquette.

So, we saluted back.

"Give me a ring" were Dad's parting words to Mr Butterworth upon reaching the Beach Road Divisional Police Station. They then saluted a 'Goodbye' to one another. Mr Butterworth with Patty in tow turned about-face and walked up the steps leading into the station.

I had often heard my parents use the expression, "I'll give you a ring" or "Give me a ring" to their friends and associates, or even heard those people tell my parents they would be giving them a ring.

What ring? Did they each have to go along to a goldsmith's shop to buy a gold ring to be given away? In this case, my parent's fingers would be heavily adorned with all manner of gold and silver rings.

It took me the better part of a year and a half—nobody said I was a fast learner -- to pose the question to my parents, who expressed uproariously great humour at the query.

They explained that 'ring' was an informal way of referring to a telephone call.

Talk about laughing out loud.

4

CHARITY REALLY BEGINS AT HOME

There aren't many parents from the 1950s and 1960s who understood the psychological trauma inflicted upon a child when *they* decided that treasured toys are no longer required, nor treasured, by the child.

"But they are MINE!" I wailed at my Dad, who in obeying orders, was handing over a huge gunny sack containing my toys, to a Malay woman in charge of a children's Home in Singapore.

"But you will receive *pahala* child..." she volunteered with a broad smile revealing she needed serious orthodontic remedial work.

"Yes, Girl, you will receive *blessings* from Heaven above," my Dad reiterated in English. Dad was a senior ranking police officer. But his orders were given by my mother, not his Commanding Officer.

"I've told you many times before, Girl, always remember you are privileged," he said, trying his best to look empathetically at my distress as far as is possible for an otherwise stern-faced military officer, but in doing so, failing miserably. The alternative, had he withdrawn the donation, would not have availed him a peaceful life over the next few weeks, or longer. He had to answer for a lot to my mother, and this would have invariably cost him another trip to the Children's Home, appearing there in abject humility, this time with my mother in tow to ensure the job was done precisely according to her directions.

The Malay woman, who was in her early thirties and had her thick black hair coiffed into a neat bun secured at the back of her head with a faux tortoise shell *cucuk sanggul*. Most Malay women possessed full heads of long, luxurious hair — considered an attractive attribute for a Malay. The *cucuk sanggul* is a hair adornment, usually made out of real or faux tortoise shell or from a highly polished glossy piece of coconut shell and used to hold up their long hair in a bun at the back of their heads. In those days, Malay women did not subscribe to wearing the *hijab*, the Islamic head scarf, as they do now.

She ushered us into the Visitors' Room in the Home and invited us to be seated. During the course of her conversation with Dad, she explained that the children in the Home were not orphans but had been abandoned by their still-living parents who for some reason or other, decided that having children was a jolly good way to justify birth control.

A young girl, whose age must be close to my eight years, entered the room bearing a tray of two glasses of orange cordial and some sugar-coated biscuits. She set the tray down carefully on the simple wooden coffee table and with her eyes lowered, started to retreat backwards, but not without first taking the opportunity of casting a furtive glance at the sack of toys in the room. I distinctly remember her subtle look of amusement at the sight of my Barbie Doll's bald head poking up from the top of the sack. I had taken great pains to shave off all the doll's hair before it, too, was cast into the sack of toys. Considering that the Barbie Doll was only introduced in Singapore in the early 1960s, my Barbie was still very much a prized *must-have* toy. After all, if I couldn't have and enjoy my Barbie Doll, then no one else should.

There must have been the equivalent of a high-speed internal communication network in the Home, even for in those days, because no sooner had the girl left the room, than there was the sound of a light thunder of feet cascading down the wooden stairs in the main hall. The Visitors Room door opened slightly and five heads, one on top of the other, suddenly appeared, curiously peering through the opening. They might have been curious, but they were silent, well-behaved children who knew their place and understood the merits of good behaviour residing in a Children's Home.

Whilst Dad and the Malay lady engaged in small chatter, I slunk out of my chair, without partaking of any of the refreshments, in protest at the imminent serious violation of my personal property. Writhing silently out of an armchair, and hopeful of avoiding detection, was the norm for well-bred young children in those days; to move about within a confined space without causing distraction or interrupting adults engaged in conversation. Rising gracefully on our own from an adult-sized armchair for an eight-year-old would otherwise be virtually impossible; simply because our feet would not have touched the ground, so a well-executed short-projected leap would have been the order of the day. If, however, while getting out of a chair, one was to get stuck through an unfortunate miscalculation of the trajectory, we would be expected to remain silent and wait for the equivalent of a pregnant pause in the conversation, before we were permitted to let out a very meek, "Excuse me, please."

Today's children, whose parents regard their precious offspring as little 'princes' and 'princesses' without possessing the blindest bit of a blue blood endorsement, simply scream their lungs out so that everyone, short of a couple of tribesmen in Outer Mongolia, would hear them and immediately respond to their demands, fawning over them incessantly.

MY FATHER IS POLICE, LAH!

I walked towards the doorway towards the five storeyed *heads*, all of which retracted with alarming alacrity upon seeing me approach. I smiled at them and gave a short wave of my hand as if to say "Hello, I'm friendly and I don't bite." The girl, who had served the drinks, came forward to greet me once I closed the room door behind me. Even as an eight-year-old, I knew to close doors behind me as my mother groomed us into remembering to always do this.

"Close the door! You don't live in a tent!" she would bellow.

Shortly afterwards, the rest gathered enough courage to serve as her backup, once they had assured themselves that I was a congenial child.

"Can you speak English?" I asked the girl 'Chief'.

"*Boleh,*" she replied softly in Malay. She had comprehended the question to give the appropriate answer, "Can", but entered a state of confusion with the choice of language. Which part of "*speak English*" didn't she understand? At this rate, it could well turn out to be a conversation between a duck and a chicken.

"What's your name?" I persisted in English. She first looked around at her friends and without perceiving apparent warning signals from them said,

"My name is Mary." She then pointed to a few others and said, "This is Ben, my brother. That is Sue, Joe, Siti, Osman, Devi, Gopal" and several other names, which I fundamentally heard and acknowledged but neglected to register for memory retention. There is only so much that an eight-year-old can be expected to adhere to at any given time.

It is a wonder that even at age eight, I was able to detect the wanting look on these children's faces. They certainly did not look as though they were starving for nourishment. They were dressed in adequate clothing and footwear, obviously courtesy of some benevolent persons' charity, and were neat in appearance, with clean fingernails. Being a policeman's daughter, I inherited from my father no less the skill of keen observation at a young age to even observe the cleanliness of others' fingernails, compounded also on account of my mother being regimental in checking her own children's level of hygiene and appearance. And behaviour. But short of each other's company, these children did not have much entertainment, if any. Television was an unaffordable luxury in those days, let alone having one in a Children's Home. We had a black and white set at home, but not many others would have had one in Singapore at that time. Thankfully, mobile phones had not yet been invented and the mention of the word WhatsApp could have easily been regarded as some form of condiment.

So, to these children, toys were indeed a very welcome contribution to the Home. I then realised that my very presence with them, let alone the sackful of toys, was already a statement of gratification and honour. To them, I had instantly become a VIP. Riding upon this illustrious wave, I suddenly remembered I still had the remnants of a fruit and nut chocolate bar in my pocket, given to me earlier by my Dad, supposedly as a gratuity to cushion the impending blow. Eager to further impress and ride higher on this wave of awe, I fished it out of my pocket and foolishly offered it with an outstretched arm and then dropped the chocolate to the ground in a panic, as the children frantically reached over to grab at yet another sought-after luxury.

This sudden display of frantic behaviour spooked me, and I immediately pivoted on my heels and rushed back into the room, nestling myself between the safe latitude of my Dad's knees. He glanced down at me with a serious expression on his face – the type of expression I surmise he must use when interrogating a criminal. He then turned towards the door to try and establish what had caused this sudden rush of fear in his daughter. Behind my Dad's cool blue eyes was wisdom; he did not pretend to be unaware and he was not gullible.

On this occasion, I had not closed the door behind me. The *ruling* from my mother contained one proviso: it was all right not to close a door behind me if I was running away from something that caused me to be afraid or feel threatened. The children must have twigged to the possible outcome of my sudden bolt. They could well be in line for some form of punishment or detention if discovered and they hot-footed it away as quickly as they had appeared. Even I had to do a double take at the door to assure myself they were no longer congregated there. They had dispersed abruptly and speedily.

"*Silakan, minum anak,*" said the Malay lady, inviting me to take my drink as she gestured towards my glass of orange cordial, which had now formed two layers of liquid in the glass; the upper layer becoming a clear liquid -- a consequence of melted ice cubes. She must have come to understand what may have occurred on the other side of the door earlier and was endeavouring to distract my father's attention.

"Yes, you must take the drink, Girl, because you have to show respect to this *mak cik*. As young children, we were taught to address all adult women as *auntie* or its Malay equivalent. "These people are not as privileged here as you are at home," he added with a hint of softness in his voice. My Dad had survived two World Wars and knew the *value* of everything, as opposed to the *price* of everything. I reached for the cold drink, which had by now become a tepid drink and gulped it down hastily and in one breath, leaving two tell-tale orange blotches at the sides of my mouth, and thereafter letting slip a loud burp, which immediately drew an amused smile, displaying the crooked teeth of the Malay lady. Dad, however, shot his signature icy glare in my direction for this ill-mannered sudden emission of gastric gases. "She's got a belly like a bellows!" my mother used to quip. A loud belch such as this one is only permissibly emitted by pot-bellied Indian coolies or their Chinese counterparts after a hefty *banana-leaf curry tiffin* when it would then be universally accepted as a gastronomical compliment to the cook. I thereupon hastily mumbled an apology and bowed my head in abject disgrace.

Dad then got up and so did the lady. She stretched out her hands in the invitation to clasp my Dad's hands, as a mark of respect and giving *Salaam*, the Islamic greeting of Peace, to him, and he reciprocated. This was the traditional and cultural norm amongst the ethnic Malays in those days—it was acceptable for a female to clasp her hands with a male's hands as a mark of respect and greeting of *Salaam*, particularly if the male person was highly esteemed.

This would be deeply frowned upon, nay penalised even, in some Islamic countries today. Such an action in Singapore would be taboo between Islamic Malay members of opposite sexes and considered *haram* or forbidden, between the parties.

How did this gracious ethnic traditional and cultural custom, turn into a forbidden ruling in one fell sweep?

Who am I to question such a transition?

5

FOR THE LOVE OF CHILDREN

Dad took my hand and we walked out of the main hall, with the Malay lady a few paces behind. We proceeded towards the verandah and down the few steps to the porch where Daeri, my Dad's driver and batman, was waiting for us in the car.

Daeri was formerly a beat patrol constable seconded from the Police Force to serve as an aide to my Dad. As soon as he saw us approach, he leapt out of the driver's seat to open the front passenger's door for my Dad and gently guided me to the rear door of my Dad's Austin Wolseley 1500. To Daeri, I was the daughter he never had. He was extremely devoted, protective, and doting, often standing between my mother and me, when she was armed with a rattan cane to mete out punishment for some errant activity I had supposedly committed. Daeri was also Malay. With a name like Daeri, my Dad assessed that Daeri was indigenous to Java. The Javanese were thought of as being gentle, soft-spoken, and hardworking.

Dad had a hypothetical behavioural science theory of the cultural characteristics of all the other servants in our house, each depending on their origin.

I looked out of the car window as we drove off from the Home. Mary, her brother Ben, and the rest of the group suddenly reappeared, like something out of a David Copperfield performance. They stood at the verandah behind the Malay lady to wave goodbye. And thank you, I expect.

"You know, you should not make such a fuss when Mum gives away your old toys and clothes. You have so many, and you should learn to share with children who don't have," my Dad started to say as we drove off, in hopes of lifting my sullen mood.

"But she doesn't ask me first!" I retorted. "Yet she won't even allow us to open a tin of chocolates without us asking her permission. So then I don't need to ask for permission either?" I moaned.

"Ask permission for what?" Dad responded quizzically.

"To give away all your things. Does this mean that I can give away all your things and Mum's things to anyone I like, without asking your permission first?" I retaliated sullenly. This outburst rendered Dad speechless. I expect at this stage of his and my life, it was a remark such as this one that might have inclined Dad to conclude I had, indeed, the makings of a lawyer. A criminal lawyer, at that.

I sat quietly in the car with my head bowed, looking extremely dejected at having been relieved of my precious toys. I hardly said a word afterwards and Dad only knew too well, that this would herald a tearful episode—my usual tactic of emotional blackmail. I could feel Dad's guilt and remorse at having brought me, his little daughter, to such an emotional breakdown.

On occasions like this, it is seemingly required that we should be filled with a sense of charity, humour, equilibrium or all three.

I never ever found out the name of that Malay lady.

This first incidental meeting at the Children's Home was the catalyst several years later that led my father to become actively involved with the management and administration of the Home. The initial building was a large double-storey colonial bungalow on two acres of manicured gardens on Tomlinson Road, which in those days was charmingly picturesque on prime land in downtown Singapore. All a bit old-fashioned, some might agree, but today, Tomlinson Road is still prime land but without the charm and ambience of the 1960s. The tranquil and picturesque ambience of grand old houses is now replaced with monstrosities of concrete edifices serving as residential high-rise luxury apartments but without the blindest bit of aesthetic sense, sacrificing elegance and majesty for sheer extravagance and stark ostentation.

Several years following his voluntary management and administration services for the Home, my father was elected chairman of the Governing Committee. He held the position for nearly a quarter of a century and he probably witnessed a turnover of more than two hundred children accommodated, educated, and nurtured within its walls. This service to the community did not go unrecognised; he received the Public Star Medal in recognition of it and a tribute to his selfless efforts in devoting his personal time and irrepressible energy, to improving the quality of life of these hapless children. It was generally agreed my father was largely instrumental in pioneering the transition of the children's educational process. It was a transition from a homegrown education system to public government-subsidised schools to foster integration with other schoolchildren. He also championed most of the school's fund-raising activities, the proceeds going to medical fees, tuition, amenities, school uniforms, and so on. He helped raise money to buy two school buses.

I often heard him reply jocularly when asked how many children he had in his family.

"Around thirty," would be his witty reply.

ROWENA HAWKINS

After the visit to the Home and as compensation for my losses, Dad took me to the Magnolia Milk Bar for a chicken pie and a packet of fresh Magnolia milk. This was always a hit insofar as comfort food was concerned, especially the ubiquitous Magnolia brand triangular-shaped waxed packet of milk. It was quite a novelty in packaging in those days, not to mention the creamy-tasting milk. It tasted better than any brand of powdered milk concoction, even if the taste of a powdered milk drink was enhanced with a generous drizzling of sweetened condensed milk. The latter only served its true purpose, drizzled lavishly over the top of *ice kacang*, a local dessert featuring shaved ice peaked over a buffet of preserved fruits and jellies or poured as a sweetening agent in locally brewed *kopi tiam* coffee, the consistency of which often could warrant the use of a fork and knife to cut through. Traditional Chinese coffee shops in Singapore still exist today and are still known by their Hokkien-style jargon *Kopi Tiam*.

There were not many free-range cows back then, because Singapore did not have all that much available land for grazing or large-scale dairy farms. Those few who did rear cows for milk in their *kampongs*, or villages, did not have high-tech modern facilities for pasteurising. The so-called dairy farmers were usually of South Indian descent and dressed in their signature rolled-up *dhotis*. These are long, white, cotton skirt-like loincloths and are still favoured amongst the South Indians. These *dhoti-clad* dairy farm peddlers were a common sight on the roads along the perimeter of today's Little India, hawking their bottles of fresh milk on tricycle carts. Sometimes, the very cows that so graciously provided the milk were also harnessed to serve as beasts of burden to tow the milk carts. These cows were not Friesian cows, nor did they resemble anything remotely close to the healthy and robust variety of dairy cows featured on the labels of popular imported milk powder brands. These bovines were conspicuously underfed with their hindquarters protruding grotesquely, and sagging bellies supporting their drooping over-milked, extremely muddy-looking udders. In fact, they looked like bizarre creatures fashioned out of a Tim Burton movie.

To any South Indian living in these *kampongs*, these creatures were unrestrained and sacred; so sacred that any likelihood of receiving good nourishing fodder, tender loving care, or a bath was a definite 'maybe'. As a sorry state of compromise, these animals could roam freely without hindrance as long as they did not encroach on the neighbouring property of a Chinese or Malay, or another Indian.

I expect any child who was nurtured on this variety of milk either developed immunity to several strains of streptococcus bacteria well into adulthood or else, the mortality rate of infant deaths in these *kampongs* would skyrocket. Another common feature of these South Indian milk peddlers was the indispensable lighted *cheroot* – a roll of local tobacco fashioned into a cigar with both ends open -- dangling precariously out of a corner of their mouth. It was not uncommon for the *cheroot* to take leave of its position in the peddler's mouth, whenever the peddler rode over an unexpected pothole or bump in the road. Then the peddler, giving no heed whatsoever to the consequences of his pause to the traffic in front of or behind his cart, nor anything other than his departed *cheroot*, would simply brake, assail passersby with a barrage of Tamil profanities, disembark and retrace his footsteps to where the oh-so-precious cigar had dropped. Very often, it was not just the *cheroot* that would take leave of the peddler's person. The *dhotis* are traditionally wound not all that tightly around their waists in order to facilitate a certain freedom of movement to pedal their carts. In the event of any sudden moves in the wrong direction, the peddler's privates could well earn themselves an airing. Without the easy availability of TV and other technological inventions in the 1960s, the general *kampong* public had to make do with such coarse forms of entertainment.

My mother did commission one such fresh-milk peddler to deliver two milk bottles to our house, daily. Not bothering to address him by his real name, she simply called him "Appu", another unfortunate-sounding name like Ah Chwee, sounding like someone sneezing. South Indians usually have exceptionally long tongue-twister names. I expect this chap must have had a name like Appumaniasamy *s/o (son of)* Murugasamy, which my mother unilaterally shortened to Appu. The name stuck.

Appu could best be described as looking like an Aryan version -- the real meaning of *Aryan* and not Hitler's version — of Groucho Marx. He wore thick round, black-rimmed spectacles confirming his seriously challenged eyesight. He often mistook the fresh milk bottles for his bottles of *thairoo,* which was a pungent variety of Indian sour milk curd, earning him an overly animated berating from our cook whenever he got it wrong. His apparent myopia conveniently gave him the advantage of feigning pure innocence, if and when he short-changed the cook when payment was made.

It was never ascertained whether his hair was real, or a home-made toupee. It consisted of a black mop of greasy-looking fibrous hair carefully centre-parted and white in the middle, all the way to the back of his head. This was secured by an almost white, rolled-up towel bandaged around his forehead. This secured the supposed hairpiece in place, and also served as a mop to catch beads of perspiration trickling down to his eyes that could further impede his vision. All in all, this hairpiece resembled a dead skunk sprawled on top of his head. He had growing on his upper lip probably the most luscious salt-and-pepper moustache I have ever seen on anyone. I overheard him telling our cook that he carefully pomaded his moustache every night with *ghee*, an Indian cooking fat, clarified butter, with a strong odour and flavour, before going to sleep, to keep it looking luscious and moist.

Why? I thought to myself. Is he going to eat it?

Well, if he did not, some rodent might.

I expect one may reasonably wonder why my mother, being so punctilious about virtually everything, would want to purchase unsanitary milk from an equally unhygienic-looking pot-bellied peddler, whose customary mode of greeting would always be accompanied by a throaty *hawk*.

Well! Ceylon Tea simply does not work with milk powder, does it? Needless to say, this variety of fresh milk and their bottles were always scrupulously boiled, twice over, prior to consumption.

And nobody in our household ever died of cholera, typhoid, or dysentery, come to think of it.

6

Celebrations and Party Events

Birthday parties were Events. This meant the temporary installation of several varieties of playground equipment, courtesy of the Fraser & Neave Company, which also supplied the sugar-overloaded soft drinks. These soft drink varieties include Orangeade, Ice Cream Soda, Cherryade, and Sarsaparilla (Sarsi for short). Sarsi was my least favourite as its taste reminded me of the smell of Dad's boot polish — not that I ever engaged myself to taste Dad's boot polish. These soft drinks are still being produced today by the same company. The General Manager of F & N also happened to be a Freemason, as was Dad, so I expected the drinks and equipment were obtained at extremely competitive rates. Steel children's tables and chairs painted in cheerful bright shades of red, green, yellow, and blue were included in the deal. Colonial bungalows were blessed with spacious ground-level verandahs, where the seating arrangements were primarily concentrated.

No less than 150 children would be invited, consisting of fellow classmates, schoolmates, and the children of my parents' friends and peers. Even the children from the Home would be in attendance, and they would arrive in a chartered bus commissioned by Dad. The servants' children were also permitted to participate in the celebrations and general party fever. My mother would act as the majordomo of the festivities, orchestrating the children's activities and directing the general duties of the servants to do all the fetching and carrying, their scurrying about resembling the actions of newly slaughtered chickens without heads. The party food would be catered by the Magnolia Milk Bar. Where else? This meant chicken pies, curry puffs, and cream horns were availed in abundance, as were our own homemade jellies and sandwiches. The birthday cakes had to be cutting-edge, state-of-the-art creations. Whilst there are such creations of master workmanship cakes conjured up by celebrity chefs today, with beautiful or bizarre architectural designs and flavours, in the 1960s, cake ingredients were rather basic and in short supply. Such imaginative intricacies as ice cream cakes were unheard of—especially for the tropics. An ice cream birthday cake could have ended up as an ice cream birthday pudding, with the candles forming an infused ingredient inside the pudding by the time the birthday song was sung.

As with her endeavours to source imaginative birthday cakes, my mother would also go to great pains to create and sew my extremely creatively designed birthday frocks. She was an expert self-taught seamstress and could stitch up a fancy frilly girl's frock in two days, given that she was a full-time career woman. It proved a challenge for her to create a state-of-the-art birthday frock for me every year.

It was only when I was old enough to apply a serious form of an analytical evaluation that I arrived at a simple deduction; all that creativity and master workmanship was intended to elicit compliments from her lady peers praising her dressmaking capacity and skills. To be fair, we both gained merit—I looked good, and she would earn the, "Oh, your mummy sewed this dress? She's SO clever!" compliment.

And then there were the presents—loads and loads of them. My mother, ever endeavouring to be politically correct in the eyes of her social peers, would make us sit down and write thank you notes to each and every person who gave a present. In the card, our handwritten contents had to painstakingly describe how lovely the present was, or delicious, if it happened to be edible, and how grateful we all were that they could attend the birthday party. I could never understand why she insisted that we had to begin with the words "thank you" when these words were already glaringly printed on the front face of every card. Perhaps in those days as well, people suffered from attention deficit/hyperactivity disorder and were unable to capture the essence of the card and its purpose at first sight of the first two words printed on the front. And if the handwriting was untidy and ugly, I had to start again from scratch. Do you have any idea how tiring and dreary it must be for an eight-year-old to write at least fifty thank-you note cards? And that number could significantly increase if the handwriting deteriorated, as was often the case by the time twenty cards were written, or if the fountain pen blotched ink all over the card or whatever other disaster could likely occur. And let me tell you that our primary school standard issue Rotax pens were not designed for industrial strength high usage -- often becoming frustrating on or before the thirty-fourth word was written.

Perhaps it was Dad's benevolent genes that made me share all my birthday presents with the servants' children. In fact, I would find more practical use of the wooden or cardboard boxes than the contents themselves. Merina and Sabariah became the proud owners of dollhouses, colouring books, board games, and eventually, all the Enid Blyton story books, Beano and Dandy comic annuals after I had read them. In the meantime, we converted drinks crates and cardboard boxes into donkey carts, attaching the wheels from our old disused perambulators to the crates' undersides. Daeri would construct the steering mechanism from some rope and another cartwheel.

Just because you have a donkey cart does not necessarily mean you have a donkey. We needed a two-horse-powered engine to drive the cart. And as we were not allowed a pony, or for that matter, a donkey on the premises, let alone a horse, the two hp motor engines took the form of Merina and Sabariah pushing from behind, whilst Jaafar acted as the traffic policeman. His job was directing the general speed and flow of traffic and issuing cigarette paper traffic summons if the girls pushed me into and beyond the parameters of Dad's prized orchid plants or into a drain. It is very hard to see where you're going if you're pushing a cart with all your might, with your head down, and you are behind the cabin with the driver obstructing more than eighty per cent of your view.

A very tall coconut tree in our garden bore the orange variety of king coconuts. The trunk must have been more than sixty feet tall, but this did not deter us from seeing who could climb highest up the tree trunk. Children know no fear of danger. I invariably would beat the others—perhaps being born in the Year of the Monkey had something to do with it. In fact, there was really no need to climb up the tree to pluck coconuts because the coconuts would fall to the ground anyway. Miraculously the coconuts never fell on anyone's head—not even Kebun's bald pate mercifully; otherwise, it would have killed him on the spot.

In addition, Kebun would commission the services of a South Indian coolie, whom we nicknamed '*Monyet*' being the Malay word for 'monkey' because he had one. We, however, gave the monkey a more dignified name. 'Marmaduke'. Zubaidah pronounced it as 'Mama-doh'. The monkey was trained to shinny up coconut trees on command from Monyet, pluck the coconuts, and hurl them to the ground. There was no particular methodology nor an organised system of Marmaduke's shotput throws. Thus, for the sake of minimising the unfortunate incidence of any casualties, we confined ourselves to observing Marmaduke's antics from the safety of the bungalow's verandah.

My parents loved to dance. Being a former ballerina, Mum was light on her feet, and Dad, who was trained at military college to excel in ballroom-style dances, was an extremely elegant dancer, cutting a rather dapper figure in black tie attire or his official Police Mess Kit. They were always in attendance at Police Gala Balls, Freemasons' Ladies' Nights and other private social functions hosted by their colonial friends and peers. Every now and then, Mum would insist that a reciprocal Dinner-and-Dance be hosted at our bungalow, usually in celebration of either her or Dad's birthday or their wedding anniversaries. The main living room, with all the furniture, moved away, was large enough to accommodate about twenty to thirty couples, and Dad would commission the Junior Police Officers Band to provide the ballroom dance music, and the Masonic Club's kitchen chefs and staff provided the catering and waiting services. Our driveway was long enough for a number of cars to be parked, and those that arrived late were parked along the road outside our front gate. Dad, being a police officer, did not need to worry about traffic summons being issued against his guests' cars. Traffic rules were pretty much laissez-faire then, as there was not that much motorised traffic on the roads anyway. The attendants would all congregate at the servants' quarters behind to socialise with the servants.

My mother was wily enough to ensure that invitations also went out to the other neighbours in the row of bungalows, including Father Long and his portly wife from the Methodist kindergarten next door, to guarantee no disruptions to the Event arising through noise complaints from the neighbours. And Father Long being present served as a double bonus — the Event was also blessed.

We children dressed in our party clothes and politely greeted the arriving guests, in a live illustration of Tez's and Corina's very well-behaved children, thereafter, to be seen only and not heard. I would be dressed in one of my mother's birthday frock sartorial creations — usually, the most recent one, as the previous years' frocks would have already been given away. My long and wavy hair would be tied up with a ribbon and knotted into a bow at the crown of my head to resemble Alice in Wonderland. Despite the tropical heat, frilly socks and closed Clarks leather shoes had to complete the ensemble. Mum believed in a calculated form of dressing for style to attract attention and not for the more practical purposes of comfort, even if it involved dress eccentricities without the slightest regard for the tropical heat. Azi would be dressed in a long-sleeved shirt with a DIY self-fix bowtie and knickerbocker-length trousers. He, too, had to wear socks with his lace-up leather shoes.

"Is wearing socks in the sweat-infused tropical heat a mandatory article of attire?" I hear you ask.

"Only if one considers the prospect of sweaty feet in a pair of leather shoes without socks, or a resulting bout of athlete's foot, a savoury consequence to be smelled!" I hear myself answer.

A school of thought dictates that if your parents underwrite the cost of your clothes, you are obliged to dress as they please, not you. This would be an acceptable arrangement if one's parents were savvy about sartorial looks, whereas children from parents who weren't ended up looking like miniature frumps in the case of a girl and a wuss in the case of a boy. I had to extend my hand and curtsey to each guest, whilst Azi had to bow waist down, with one arm folded in front of his waist and the other folded behind his waist. Sometimes, we received a short verbal response from the guests, usually asking what our names were. The comments, mostly compliments, would be directed at my beaming Mum, "Corrina, your children are SO well-behaved and absolutely charming!"

As soon as the formalities were over, we escaped to the servants' quarters to join Daeri and the gang of syces, or attendants, to play with our children's fireworks and other accessories, consisting of sparklers, rockets, and candle-lit paper lanterns. Daeri was charged with ensuring we lit the rockets carefully and the lit lanterns did not catch fire whilst we, in single file, paraded with them up and down the garden, weaving in between the parked cars.

We would then be rounded up, ushered upstairs for our bath, and then got into our pyjamas, for bedtime was at 8:00 p.m. sharp. However, on party nights, our ayahs sometimes permitted us to creep down the stairs and peep through the staircase's wooden double doors at the goings-on of the adults downstairs. By about half past eight, the overflowing liquor consumption would be starting to produce consequential results, and this correspondingly increased the decibel count of male voices. My Dad's gramophone or the musical numbers performed by the Police Band would be blaring away, and couples would be floating around our spacious living room, dancing to the strains of Frank Sinatra and Big Bands' ballroom dance music. Exuberant bouts of laughter would be on the rise; bowties, jackets and high-heeled shoes would take leave of their owners, and couples could be seen in dalliance, sometimes too close for polite society's comfort, and not necessarily with their spouses.

The morning after heralded the opportunity to run downstairs to see who could get the best, and the most, left-over party pickings — empty cigarette tins, which served to hold our

MY FATHER IS POLICE, LAH!

individual collection of *kuti-kuti* and sometimes, the odd fallen bracelet charm, handkerchief, a hand fan, the odd shoe and even an evening purse or two. *Kuti-Kuti* were small plastic tokens in the shapes of animals and everyday objects used in a children's game. One token is flicked forward in short movements towards the opponent's token in an alternate sequence to land on top of the other's token. The winner would then acquire the loser's token. Dad was then a smoker. Brand 555 or John Player Special brands, both of which were packaged in tins, were his choice. Truth be told, I can probably attest to having my first cigarette when I was two years old. Whilst sitting on Dad's lap one day, he rested his cigarette on an ashtray within a short reachable distance from me and which my ever-inquisitive fingers could easily retrieve. Then I drew a hefty puff from the lit cigarette. My coughing and gagging were so vigorous that they drew the immediate attention of my mother, who practically flew down the stairs to berate my father. Dad could have considered the notion of quitting smoking then and there.

Hari Raya Puasa and Hari Raya Haji, both being the Muslim Eid Festivals, were jubilantly celebrated at our house, particularly as the servants were mostly Muslims. My parents would host an Open House for their friends and associates, and this involved in-house catering of a colossal magnitude. The kitchen's largest steel and ceramic cauldrons would be deployed, and food would be prepared in the courtyard rather than in the commodious kitchen. Mum insisted all the food be traditionally cooked on wood fires or charcoal fire stoves, which invariably produced a high volume of smoke and fumes best dispersed in the open air. Zubaidah would be in her element; the other servants were roped into the food preparation extravaganza, and they, in turn, would recruit relatives and other folk from their *kampongs*. The courtyard and servants' quarters would be buzzing with activity.

Zubaidah would be cutting a prominent figure in the middle of the courtyard around the servants, standing with her feet apart, arms akimbo and squawking directives at the servants. She would also grab this opportunity to dress up, which in itself was a testament to sacrificing elegance and beauty for extravagance and ostentation. It has been said that ostentation does not necessarily beget style; in Zubaidah's case, it totally wrecked it. She would ensure both arms were bedecked with gold bracelets and bangles, virtually encompassing a wrist-to-elbow span. Her head would be slightly bent down in a painstakingly obvious effort to support the myriad hoops of gold chains of various lengths, drooping with amulets and pendants. So much for always being well-dressed but the keep-it-simple adage also applies. The usual white caked face powder and the dark circles of a combination of dark eye shadow and black eyeliner would be embellished with two bright pink pats of rouge on both cheeks haphazardly applied to make it appear as if someone had recently slapped her face on both sides. The ultimate facial garnish would be the garish crimson lipstick applied in an elliptical form that neither necessarily followed the actual contours of her mouth. If captured on camera, I fancy her physiognomy could easily be mistaken for that of a female giant panda wearing lipstick. If captured during the night in a dark alley, however, one could hypothesise that an overly made-up, over-dressed, middle-aged, overweight woman wearing a goldmine in jewellery could either be arrested or mugged if she did not first scare the living daylights out of her accosters. She would also totter precariously on the 1960s version of stiletto-heeled open-toed sandals, displaying her chubby toes painted with red nail lacquer. Not dissimilar to the lipstick around her mouth, the nail lacquer also would not be applied within the contours of her toenails. In today's physiotherapy analyses, a large woman trying to balance her overly generous body on very high needle heels is not only uncomfortable but also asking for acute spinal sclerosis.

The most consequential part of the event for us children, however, was playing with the readily available firecrackers that Dad gave us. There were several varieties: the smaller coloured bunches which when lit, emitted a far milder explosion than the larger bright red variety. As the bright reds gave off a louder explosion and therefore posed a more dangerous alternative to the smaller coloured ones, Dad only bought us one or two packets of the red firecrackers. This precious ammunition, we saved for one specific agenda—to scare the living daylights out of Zubaidah. Amid her grandioso culinary orchestration, she would invariably require several lavatory breaks. Azi and I would carefully tail her at a distance to establish the expected duration of the lavatory visit. If a bad smell like a decaying dead rat emanated from the lavatory, duly accompanied by heaves and groans of varying scales of effort, then this was an opportune moment when audacity took over from good behaviour. As I was smaller in stature, Azi would instruct me to creep up to the lavatory and remove Zubaidah's footwear from the vicinity of the door. So, with one hand holding my nose, I reached out with the other outstretched hand to take the high-heeled sandals and tiptoe around the corner to place them at a safe distance so she would not trip over them when she exited the lavatory. Well, that was one line of thought. More importantly, if the truth be told, the real purpose of this precautionary measure was so that she could not reach for them to use as missiles to be hurled at us. Azi would then lie in wait for the sound of the lavatory flushing before lighting the firecrackers and carefully placing the explosives outside the lavatory door. Then, stand well back.

BAH-DAH-BAH-DAH-BAH-DAH-BAH-DAH-BAH-DAH!

the ear-splitting noise of firecrackers resounded. The reaction was always predictable—an ear-splitting *Aiiieeeeeyyaaah*! screech from within the lavatory followed by a barrage of gibberish and exclamations with no particular language, sequence, or meaning, "*O Mah-mie Gochok Babu, O Mak Puchok*", and so on, repeated over and over, being the usual. As soon as the lavatory door opened, Azi and I would put on our most cherubim faces and point to the nearest servant bystander—usually, it was the hapless Kebun—to whom Zubaidah would march up sans footwear and twist his ear, accompanied by a mouthful of expletives in their own Boyanese and Banjarese dialects. I cannot translate these expressions to maintain an agreeable level of decorum within this narrative.

Kebun was obsequious and never fought back. I hazard a guess that above the seemingly thick coating of respectability for his spouse, he must have felt deeply sorry for her. Therein lies the exorbitant toll of the marriage covenant of "…forsaking all others, for better or worse, in sickness or in health, till death do us part".

As a Muslim, Kebun had the Islamic right to have four wives. But one wife was trouble enough, why multiply one's trouble four-fold? Kebun surely championed the personification of the Latin phrase, *Fidelis Usque Ad Mortem,* Faithful unto Death.

7

THE PRINCE & HEIR

As the only son and heir, my brother, *Tuanku Mohammad Quolam Asad Sabir Zainabdul,* whom we called 'Azi' was given five official names, not including the royal title, *Tuan*. They must have been so overwhelmed by the blessing of a firstborn grandson and heir that every living elder on both sides of the parents must have insisted upon chipping in with a name for the poor boy. That not being enough, my parents then christened him with an additional 'pet' name for good measure.

This appears to be pattern of protocol amongst Asian cultures, more so amongst royal circles. This same principle was applied when I was born three years later. While I had three officially given names, none of these was used to address me at home. Instead, I was given another pet name, Girlie. This name was used throughout my childhood and teenage years, and I only outgrew it when I reached adulthood.

Azi was the name we used back then. And we still do. Fortunately, the school he attended, which served as both his primary and secondary school, did not insist on name badges, otherwise, my brother's name badge would have overshot the front of his uniform and reached his forearm. Reading his name badge would be like watching a tennis game—eyes darting from left to right—Tuanku Mohammed Quolam Asad Sabir Zainabdul.

Azi was, as best expected from an older brother and prince, spoilt. It was not his fault; he did not ask to be spoilt—it was part and parcel of the princely package. As such, he would get away with blue murder, mostly because Mum had the annoying and insensible habit of hitting first and asking questions later. Azi would run rampant with a box of crayons, using the walls as his drawing board. Unfortunately, he was no artist prodigy, otherwise his efforts might have been appreciated as a mural on the walls, rather than a colossal mess. So when Mum came home from work and saw the crayon scribbling on the walls, there would be this loud screech in an alternating low and then high tone.

"Gir-leeee!...A-zeeeee!" would be the call to report to her at once. Azi, having been born in the Year of the Snake, had an acute sense of cunning and wiles—plus, he had the advantage of being three years older than me. Upon hearing Mum's call in that specific tone, he knew it meant trouble. So he always pushed me forward and said, "Girl, you go see what Mum wants, she called your name first." And I was ever-trusting of my older brother, not to mention how younger siblings tend to robotically follow the instructions of older ones. So I would go skipping forward unsuspectingly to Mum, only to be the first recipient of a well-placed smack over the head, followed by my high-pitched wail.

"WHO asked you to scribble on the walls like this!?" she would bellow until the servants and their children also would come running to participate as a built-in rent-a-crowd. The servants' children would form a line of varying heights along the verandah and peer over the large grilled windows to see what the melodrama was all about, whilst their parents would come forward and explain to Mum, albeit too late, that it was her son standing over there at a very safe distance no less and feigning a forlorn look with well-practised woeful eyes, who was the real culprit. She would then swing around to glare at Azi and shout,

"Azi-boy!" (the suffix was superfluous as we all knew he was not a girl) "Did you do this?" to which my brother would reply softly, "Yes, Mum," and then quickly add in a louder defiant voice, "but it was Girlie's crayons!"

At moments like this, a pair of horns and an arrowhead tail would suddenly sprout upon Azi's person. I never received any apology or compensation for being wrongfully punished for the crimes I never committed. Parents were not coached in the fine art of parenting, using soft skills; there was no parenting 'charm school' in Singapore.

They say dentist's children have the worst teeth and doctor's children have the worst illnesses. Therefore, this ought to suggest that policemen's children must be the worst crooks.

There is a sound certainty in the assurance that once you have learnt to ride a bicycle, the knowledge remains with you for life. This is also true of my brother and his skill at picking locks. He was a genius — no lock was safe from him. He could pick any lock using the barest of tools, even a large safety pin. This skill he used on many occasions as a commodity for barter with my pocket money, as a service offered to unlock Kebun's Elswick bicycle for my riding lessons. He unlocked the padlock of Mum's larder where our birthday presents, tins of chocolates and sweet biscuits were being stored, and even unlocked my parents' almirahs, or wardrobes, to ransack the contents for curious forbidden articles.

It was a Saturday night, and my parents were out. As it was Saturday, they had very likely gone to a Freemasons' Ladies Night or a Police Officers' Mess Dance Night, or some other social engagement. The servants had retired to their quarters save for our *ayahs*, who were either preening themselves before bedtime or ready to get into bed. So was I.

I suddenly heard a loud BAAM! I immediately sprang out of bed and ran out to the upper floor family lounge area, where I saw my brother in front of Dad's almirah, where he kept all his police regalia, paraphernalia, and equipment. Azi was looking deathly pale; his normal complexion is not dissimilar to that of the Ace of Spades. My father's almirah door appeared to be slightly open. To my bafflement and his own surprise, he managed to step gracefully out of an action he had mercifully blundered, which otherwise could have turned into a real tragedy.

"What was that noise?" I yelled at him.

"Nothing, nothing. Go back to sleep, or I'll tell *Ayah* that you are still playing around," came his reply. Playing around? Me? That was an understatement. Anyway, I moved towards him gingerly to see what he was holding behind his back. He gave me a threatening glare—one I knew only too well to mean that if I came any closer, I could expect a sharp smack on the head or a blow to the arm. My father's sage adage that discretion is the better part of valour must have sprung to mind because I immediately pivoted on my heels and went back to my bed, without giving the incident a second thought.

It was only very many years later that we talked about this incident, and I found out what took place that night. He had managed to pick the lock on my father's almirah, where Dad kept his service revolver under lock and key whenever he went out on social engagements. Azi had picked up the fully loaded revolver and out of curiosity—I would have put it down to sheer stupidity—aimed the barrel at the side of his forehead and pulled the trigger. Owing to the service revolver being an old-fashioned heavy weapon, and the awkwardness of holding up a gun to the side of his head, he required the use of both of his thumbs to pull the trigger. The inertia of pulling the trigger with two thumbs deflected the barrel away from his head. The shot was fired, and the bullet might have ricocheted around the lounge area somewhere. Despite desperately crawling about on his hands and knees to look for and get rid of the incriminating evidence, he could not find the spent bullet anywhere in the upstairs lounge at the time.

The upper floor lounge area of colonial bungalows was structured like an open verandah with no windows. They were architecturally designed with this open-air plan concept to allow as much air circulation as possible into the upper floor of the bungalow. Bamboo chicks were fastened to these open-air windows, and these would only be lowered during heavy rain so the upstairs lounge would not be drenched or flooded. There was also the possibility that the bullet may have just flown out of these open-air windows and landed somewhere around the garden and grounds. Despite combing the garden and grounds the following morning, Azi could not find that spent bullet. Perhaps it had been sighted as a glistening object and picked up by a minah bird out of sheer curiosity — a trait not dissimilar to that of Azi the night before. And how he talked his way into allaying my interest and the concern of the *ayah*, who also, upon hearing the noise came running out to investigate, especially when the smoking gun was still in his hand behind his back, and a thin wisp of smoke was rising up from behind him. He told me that the spent bullet was never found, at least not to his knowledge. Over the years, that remark has caused me a degree of perplexity because I was under the impression that police officers possessing firearms would have to account for each spent bullet. How did Dad account for the missing bullet? It still remains an enigma today; I never asked him.

My princely brother was the boss among the children in the

household. Although he was given a lot of licence to do whatever he liked, as long as it was not criminal, he often disregarded the essential meaning of 'criminal' in his psyche or perhaps had his own interpretation of the word.

Azi, together with his chestnut of a head, grew up to be an extremely intelligent and numerate chap with an extraordinarily high I.Q. He was subsequently invited to become a member of the local Mensa Society. How did that happen? Perhaps that bump on the head, when he was a toddler really was a good thing after all? Had I known this to be the case then, I too could have happily contributed towards several more bumps to his head, solely of course, for the purpose of aiding his mental development. He could have become a rocket scientist if he possessed the capacity to discipline his extraordinary I.Q.!

One fine day during our school term holidays and without anything new to allay his boredom, he suddenly announced that we should call the police and tell them that there were robbers in our house. Dad had a special black telephone installed in our house, the line directly linked to the Police Headquarters and was only availed to him for the HQ and his exclusive use, to have direct access to one another in the event of a dire emergency. The moment the receiver was lifted off the cradle, the HQ switchboard operator would be able to immediately identify the phone call as coming from our house. My brother, thinking himself to be a champion amongst the weak, lifted the receiver and said, "Hello, police? You had better come to our house. There are robbers here," and then quickly hung up, to the giggles and laughter from the rest of us, thinking how swell this was and that we were all being ever so smart.

Within an unexpected space of five to eight minutes, a police car drew up to our front gate and a huge police lorry with fortified grilled windows called a *Black Maria* pulled up too. To

MY FATHER IS POLICE, LAH!

this day, I do not know why it was referred to as a Black Maria. Yes, the lorry was black, but who was Maria? Words fail me in this attempt to describe our horror and panic at the sight of the police car and Black Maria arriving at our front gate. Azi quickly barked out orders, "Okay men! Quick GO! Run to the back and hide!" We were referred to as *men* because he saw us as part and parcel of his personal infantry brigade.

We scrambled about to find suitable hiding places at the back of the house. Azi hid in an old disused fridge in the courtyard; I ran to the back of the servants' quarters and hid in the lavatory, which stank of stale urine. The latch of the lavatory door was faulty, so with one hand, I had to hold my nose to block out the stench, and with the other hand, I had to hold the lavatory door shut from the inside. Merina and Sabariah, both of whom had too much *'room to let between the ears'* and not being totally familiar with the nooks and crannies of the house, simply ran to the dining room and crouched under the large dining table, which stood on four solid wooden legs with the claws of a lion. The underside area beneath the table top was completely see-through. As soon as one stood at our front doorway, the immediate and obvious direct line of vision would be to the area underneath our dining table at the dining hall. Therefore, as soon as the police constables entered the house, they first saw the dining table with the two girls cowering underneath. They were fished out, and the girls, not wanting to be unjustly chastised for something they did not orchestrate, headed straight to the disused fridge where Azi was hiding. Without being prompted to do so, Merina opened the fridge door to find him squatting inside on his haunches, with his hands covering his ears. Both girls gingerly pointed to him as the ringleader.

Azi was not the most protective of big brothers in the world. I was standing in the wrong queue when they were handing out big brothers. When he was good, he was very, very good. Ah, but when he was bad and possessed with vindictiveness, that was quite a different story. A good brother would have taken the bullet and protected his younger sibling and the other two girls. But Oh No! Not this fellow. After all, he was born in a Snake Year, so why should he absorb the blame all by himself when he could generously split it with his ever-trusting younger sister, et al.?

The next thing I heard was footsteps approaching the servants' lavatory and the sound of male voices and our *ayahs'* voices. There was a push on the door from the outside, and I retaliated with a restrained weak pushback from the inside. This see-saw action went on for a few swings until a soft male voice called out to me to come out. All I can say at this juncture is that it was a good thing that I was hiding in a lavatory, stinky as it was, because there suddenly was this urge to relieve myself when I heard the footsteps approaching.

The police fortuitously did not reprimand us. They, instead, aimed their dissatisfaction and warnings at the servants. The *ayahs* received the brunt of the reprimands for not watching over the children responsibly. Today, we children would have been exchanging high fives with one another for this great stroke of good fortune. As it turned out, this outburst of exhilaration was not going to last for long. Azi envisaged that the *ayahs* would be reporting the incident to Mum. Dad would have already heard about it through the Police HQ Reporting network before they returned home. So, this bright spark of a brother came up with yet another cunning plan. "We'll go to bed early, and when Mum comes into the room to look for us, we'll pretend to be sleeping. Then she cannot punish us if we are asleep." Us? Hello? He was using the plural tense there. Shouldn't it be, "*She cannot punish me?*" I still had not yet developed an analytical mind at the grand old age of eight, so I did not question his directive. We bathed, wolfed down our dinner and shot into bed well before our parents returned home. As soon as we heard the car pull up into the driveway, we feigned 'lights out'. It was only 5:30 p.m. Bedtime was at 8:00 p.m.

We could hear the *ayahs* talking to Mum downstairs, followed by the *clip-clop* sound of her footsteps coming up the stairs. She then stepped into the bedroom whilst Azi and I stopped breathing. After a few seconds, which seemed like a few hours when you are holding your breath, she turned and went out, much to our relief that we had escaped corporal punishment.

No, we had not. We both got a caning the next morning. As soon as we came downstairs for breakfast, she was standing in the dining room sporting that oh-so-familiar dark stern look. However, she was not wielding the dreaded long stick of polished bamboo in her right hand. So, we were gratefully relieved by this.

"WHO called the police yesterday?" Thankfully, she resorted to asking questions first this time around. Without answering, I pointed to Azi, who glared at me for rat-finking on him. "Azi-boy!" my Mum said in a tone that was blindingly restrained, not wanting to appear an ogress to her precious son, nor to the assembled jury present, "GO and bring me the cane. I'm going to beat you both with it!"

My mother's normal level of common sense appeared to have abandoned her at that moment, making her sound like a dimwit and not the most logical person in the world. Now, why would any normal person comply with an order to go forth, look for and bring forward an implement that inflicts insufferable pain, and give it to the person who is going to inflict that pain upon them? That would be like telling someone, "Kindly pass me that custard cream pie so I can ram it into your face!" Azi, seeing an opportunity to evade liability said, "I don't know where the cane is. I think Girlie threw it away last time." It was just another occasion like the one with the crayons when my brother's two horns emerged on his head and that arrowhead tail sprouted from behind. He was incorrigible. And still is.

Mum brushed past him and went to get the cane by herself; if you are going to hit someone, get the weapon yourself.

This was just one of many such occasions when Daeri, realising that I was in grave danger of unmitigated corporal punishment, came forward in my defence and subserviently approached my raging mum, endeavouring to explain that it was not I, nor the servants' children who had called the police, but that it was Azi who was the real perpetrator. "*Ma'af Mem, budak Girl 'ni 'tak bikin salah. Abang dia yang panggil polis. Girl 'ni masih mudah lagi, Mem...*" He continued pleading that the other two girls and I were just young, innocent accessories to Azi's mischief.

Azi glared at Daeri, with his eyes revealing that a diabolical and vengeful plot was being devised in his impish mind. Unlike Azi, Daeri had a halo over his head. Nonetheless, Mum decided that everyone ought to be taught a lesson, so she instructed the servants to punish their own children, and we were condemned to the cane — five strokes administered to each child on the palm of each hand.

Azi did not forget his promised revenge on Daeri for taking my side. He also was not familiar with the saying, if you intend to seek revenge on someone, dig two graves first. As an eleven-year-old with a remarkably high I.Q., he was more au fait with grown-up paraphernalia than someone twice his age. There was a rattan round table with two matching chairs situated on the front verandah, which served as Daeri's station for when he needed to polish the silver buttons on Dad's uniform or polish Dad's police boots, or just to have a rest while waiting for Dad. His wife Rukiah would make him a large mug of local black coffee and set it down on the table. This was to serve as the catalyst for carrying out Azi's retribution. Since no lock was safe from him, he picked the lock on Dad's liquor cabinet and took out a miniature bottle of whiskey and another bottle of gin. These, he decided, would be used to spike Daeri's coffee.

I heard the liquor cabinet door creak when it was opened and from where I was perched halfway up at the corner of the staircase, witnessed him removing the miniature bottles, tucking them into the pocket of his shorts and proceeding outdoors to the porch where Daeri was washing Dad's car. I kept myself well out of sight and watched what he was going to do with them — thinking at first that he was intending to experiment with the taste of a shot of whiskey and gin. I heard him making small talk with Daeri, and the rattan chairs creaked as he sat on one of them. About ten minutes later, I heard the front door, which had been ajar, close. Azi walked up the stairs nonchalantly as if the world were a stage and he was the director.

"Whaddya want?" he barked at me when he came around the corner of the staircase and suddenly caught sight of me perched mid-way up. I expect the shock of suddenly seeing me there must have triggered a guilt reaction, and hence, his aggression. Another of Dad's famous remarks, albeit contradictory to his discretion, was, "Attack is the best form of defence." This sage snippet, too, has stayed with me all my life.

"Nothing! Cannot sit here, *izzit?*" I hissed back defiantly. Knowing he would be vigilantly watching my next step, I followed him up the stairs and managed to slip away into my parent's bedroom, where Rukiah was changing the bedsheets.

In the meantime, Azi headed for the lavatory — all that diabolical sneakiness was causing a near bladder burst. I snatched the opportunity and related to Rukiah what I suspected, and she hurried down the back stairs to warn her husband. As it turned out, there was no need to do so — Daeri was a policeman. He had discreetly observed Azi trying to unscrew the apparently tight alcohol bottles' screw caps and just feigned oblivion. After Azi went indoors, Daeri took a sniff of the adulterated coffee and, upon confirming its alcoholic contents, poured the concoction into a nearby pot plant. He narrated the incident to Dad, who, after being shown the liquid, some of it remaining afloat on the soil, took a short whiff and frowned. I expect his eyebrows must have met in the middle again. He immediately called for Azi to come downstairs for an interrogation. Mum, who overheard Dad's loud and steely tone of voice, also hurried down to see what the matter was.

When Azi arrived, Dad held him firmly by the shoulder and growled very slowly and solemnly, "Son, did you pour liquor from my cabinet into Daeri's coffee?" Of course, I was squatting behind the front door with just my head poking around the door, watching and listening — a melodrama about to unfold like this was not to be missed. I had never seen Dad look so enraged; his anger was usually silent. His look with his glaring, steely blue eyes even warned Mum to remain silent. Azi said nothing; he knew Dad meant business. With his head bowed in abject humility, he nodded. Dad then applied pressure on Azi's shoulder and commanded him to kneel before Daeri. Without any hint of argument, he knelt before Daeri.

"Apologise! Don't you dare ever do this again to Daeri. DO you understand me?" Dad' thundered. The crestfallen boy nodded his head again as he asked Daeri to forgive him for his mischief. "*Ampun, Pak Cik Daeri" Azi mintak ampun,*" he cried woefully. At that moment, I could not understand why Dad got so mad about this seemingly childish prank.

It was only when Mum was consoling, and counselling Azi later, that the penny dropped. Daeri was a devout Muslim, and alcohol was absolutely forbidden amongst orthodox Muslims. Azi had not only shown disrespect for a member of Dad's staff but also committed a cardinal sin against a devout Muslim. It certainly was not Daeri's intention to create any embarrassment for Dad and bring disharmony between a father and his son. But Daeri considered Azi's actions extremely offensive to a Muslim and, correspondingly, to other Muslims, if he ever pulled this prank again on one. He nonetheless forgave this errant boy, knowing that to Azi, this was nothing more than boyish mischief.

When you choose to forgive the person who hurts you, you simultaneously take away their power. And Azi had to be taught never to do this again to anyone, let alone a Muslim.

8

Child's Horseplay

The colonial bungalows along our residential road were going to be spruced up. This meant our bungalow was going to receive a facelift. A new coat of paint was going to be applied to the entire house's exterior, and there was going to be much activity over the next few weeks. The scaffolding was made of bamboo poles, which would then be secured with rattan strips to form the framework. The coolies erecting the scaffolding around the house were astonishingly adept at securing the poles in a criss-cross design, and it is somewhat amazing how these poles could support the weight of several workmen standing on the same pole at any one time. These bamboo poles came in different sizes to facilitate the various widths and heights of the areas that had to be painted.

Azi saw an opportunity to use his creativity and engage the surplus bamboo poles lying around to serve as the pony and horse we were not allowed. Sometimes, he instructed us to take a shorter pole and stand astride it holding on to the front of the pole as the pony's reins with the other end of the pole dragging behind on the ground. And with this mechanism in place, we would gallop around the garden and grounds as his infantry brigade.

MY FATHER IS POLICE, LAH!

"C'mon, men! Forward Ho-oo!" he would bellow, and we all dutifully followed behind in single file. This was not such a bad pastime and, of course, great fun. The contracted workers never complained of us children utilising their spare bamboo poles and likewise, we were ecstatically happy to have been availed of new toys.

The pavement in front of our house stretched along the entire row of colonial bungalows, and our parents gave us permission to access the pavements, provided we stayed on them, did not venture onto the main road, and were accompanied by one of the ayahs. By the time he was eleven years of age, Azi had decided that an *ayah's* supervision was surplus to requirements, so he often took it upon himself to dictate his own actions and choices. This time around, he selected one bamboo pole, which was considerably longer than our usual pony lengths. He straddled this longer pole whilst commanding the rest of us to straddle the same pole behind him. At full strength, the long pole could accommodate five of us straddling it but manoeuvring it was not quite as easy as he anticipated, as it involved getting five children to synchronise their footsteps. The leg movement and rhythm of five riders went seriously awry, and every now and then, one of us would lose balance and topple over, which invariably dragged the other four down as well. With this apparent failure of his modus operandi, Azi commanded the other three children to dismount and instructed that they should just run behind like the old-fashioned torchbearers accompanying an English horse-drawn coach.

So, this is how we proceeded along the pavement; Azi at the head, I at mid-point and three runners behind. Trotting up the pavement in one direction was effortless, and we got as far as the Post Office at one end of the pavement. Now came the tricky bit—pivoting around to trot back to the house. This involved negotiating a 180-degree turn astride a long bamboo pole. Having no proper driving lessons nor being adept at manoeuvring tactics, Azi simply turned the 180 degrees with me, synchronising the rhythm and pace of his footsteps to follow suit, but both of us neglected to notice the Indian *kacang putih* peddler of nuts and pulses as titbits and snacks, emerging from the Post Office and approaching behind us. He unexpectedly descended the steps and appeared out of nowhere, with his tray of nuts and pulses balanced on a wound-up piece of flannel on top of his head. What happened next was inevitable. Upon negotiating the turn, the rear end of the pole struck the peddler. He toppled over, and his tray of nuts, pulses and snacks became airborne, flying in myriad directions, its contents landing all over the pavement and the main road, much to the horror of Azi, myself and the other three children with us. We were not going to hang about and be targets of the berating to follow.

"*ADEY!*" the peddler shouted as the three children scampered off. South Indian peddlers use *Adey* as a generic form of call or address. Hey, or Oi is not generally found in the Tamil vocabulary. Azi and I, as if by telepathy, dropped the pole in one swift move and ran down the pavement to our house, Azi closing and bolting our front gate behind him. It took a while for the peddler to reach our front gate, and he yelled out several *Adey's* until Ah Chwee came out to confront him at the gate. Obviously, he was looking for compensation for his losses and was shouting all kinds of Tamil expletives and calling upon a pantheon of known or unknown Hindu deities before Ah Chwee decided to emerge and put him out of his misery. Much as I admire these peddlers' entrepreneurial skills, they also ought to have deployed P.R. skills.

To aid and abet her proposed negotiation, Harris, our shop steward and also Saminah's husband, accompanied Ah Chwee to confront the peddler. Harris was a real maverick negotiator, as he would frequently be required to bargain when purchasing our groceries and whatever else. Ah Chwee, being Chinese, saw an opportunity to haggle with an Indian. She started the negotiation by telling him that if he wanted payment, then he had to scoop up every single one of the nuts and pulses that had been scattered on the pavement and bring it to her — otherwise, she would not be paying him any money at all. The Chinese astuteness and keen business acumen skills are renowned, and they are often referred to as the 'Jews of the East'. Ah Chwee, however, said this only in jest to taunt him and earn herself a small moral victory. I now wonder whether Ah Chwee had known Shakespeare's *The Merchant of Venice* and the famous quote about a pound of flesh.

Harris, in support of Ah Chwee's goading and just to pile it on even further, demanded proof from the hapless peddler that a bamboo pole from our bungalow had knocked him over. He pointed out that all of the eight bungalows in the row had both children and scaffolding around the houses. Thus, what made him so sure the bamboo pole and children were from our particular bungalow? Anyway, Ah Chwee was a kindly and charitable woman and a devotee of the deity Kwan Yin, the epitome of mercy. She did pay him an amount for his lost products and, of course, then sought reimbursement from my parents.

As usual, the ubiquitous "A-zeee!! Gir-leee!" was forthcoming with alarming alacrity as soon as Mum came home. Azi was initially cagey with his explanation. After he had worked out in his mind what he thought to be a perfectly plausible excuse, he simply told her, "Mum, the *kacang putih* man *sendiri jatuh,*" attempting to attribute sole liability to the peddler. He said the man had fallen over by himself through his own clumsiness. "We did not push him and who asked him to 'cari pasal' and get in our way when we were playing by ourselves?" Piling it on, Azi added the peddler had orchestrated his own calamity. At this precise moment, I am surprised a halo did not appear above his head since he refrained from attributing blame to me or the other three children, his usual practice.

And, oh yes, a caning followed.

A Methodist Church and kindergarten annex were next door to our bungalow, both within the same compound. School holidays were designed to bring out the mischief in us, and one of Azi's favourite pastimes was to contradict directives. As the classrooms would be vacant during school holiday, this presented a wonderful opportunity to help ourselves to various items of stationery and knick-knacks from the kindergarten classrooms.

A barbed wire fence surrounded by a dense hedgerow separated the two compounds around the entire perimeter of our garden. Some parts of the hedge were sparse, and these places conveniently provided us with a means to infiltrate the kindergarten's compound. On the other side of the hedge lay opportunities, swings, see-saws, other children's playground equipment, and a large, covered hall that served as a badminton arena or a dance hall for hire. Then there were the empty classrooms in which were stored boxes of blackboard chalk, coloured pencils and erasers and other delectable goodies of classroom stationery. The latter, of course, were more to our liking. Even though my parents ensured we had ample forms of stationery and books, as these were regularly purchased for us, the lawfully obtained ones were not as enticing as stolen property. Azi always felt a frisson of excitement when a sleight of hand to pilfer things presented itself. Forbidden fruit always tastes sweeter.

Azi would thereupon force me to wriggle through the sections of sparse hedge and barbed wire to get to the kindergarten compound, as I was the smaller of us. The other children were not in the equation because "they're too stupid," he would complain. Once in the precincts of the kindergarten, I was to go into the nearest classroom and pinch boxes of chalk, pencils, erasers, and other items. Then I was to perch on the classroom windowsill, squatting on my haunches and then hurl the stolen loot over the hedge, whereupon Azi and the other children were to catch the items as they flew over. I expressed a little concern, saying that perhaps the caretaker may be lurking around the corner and watching our pilfering.

"Don't be so stupid, Girlie. How can the caretaker be watching us like a hawk when he is as blind as a bat?" Azi berated.

The first few heists were simply a breeze. But, of course, there had to be the one occasion when the kindergarten's caretaker, an old Chinese coolie who really was blind in one eye, happened to come around the corner just as I was perched on the windowsill and had just hurled some items across the hedge. He stopped dead in his tracks, and I correspondingly froze still in my squatting pose on the windowsill.

In the meantime, Azi and the other children dispersed in all directions, speedily and abruptly, out of the incriminating zone. They hid behind some palm tree trunks in our garden, leaving me alone to deal with the caretaker. The old man glanced at me with his one good eye and then at our side of the garden in alternating sequences. I figured he was making sure that at least his good eye was not deceiving him and that what he saw was for real. He threatened to inform the resident priest, Father Long, and Dad about what was going on.

Even as an eight-year-old, I was surprised by my negotiating skills when it came to extricating myself from a tight spot. I retorted that if he did so, I would tell my father about his escapades of climbing over our hedge and stealing our ripe jack fruit, bananas, coconuts, and guavas, and also helping himself to our coconut palm leaves that he would fashion into palm leaf crosses for Palm Sunday. He didn't get permission from my parents for any of this and all our servants would attest to the same. And my father being a police officer, he could be put in jail. Nothing as drastic would happen to me as I was mere child.

He may have been blind in one eye, but he knew a real l threat when he heard one. He also knew a good deal when he was given an opportunity to strike one. Thereupon a long-standing deal was struck. He could continue with his jackfruit, bananas, coconuts, guavas, and palm leaf poaching activities without fear of reprisals, and we in exchange would receive a supply every now and then of extra bits of chalk and pencils, lawfully handed to us by the old man.

9

A Brush with the Supernatural

The most extraordinary incident, which I recall in great detail, was a profound eye-opener to me, for it introduced me to elements of the supernatural I had never before known existed. Despite there being times when I would wake up suddenly in the middle of the night and see a dwarf-like entity with coarsely chiselled facial features sitting on the side or at the foot of my bed staring at me, I could never be sure as to whether I was dreaming this. All I knew was that sudden cessation of breath and paralysis of my body movements would herald these experiences. This, in fact, was a more frightening sensation than seeing the apparition itself, as at times like this, I would mentally question myself as to whether this was how I was going to die. I would also seemingly mouth the name of my ayah to whom I would be endeavouring to call for assistance, but no sound would come out of my mouth. These occurrences would last for eight to ten seconds, and then I would suddenly snap out of it, into a conscious state. Thereafter when I called out to my ayah in a state of trepidation, she would promptly respond and come to my aid. I told her many times over about the experiences and the visions of the entity — usually, it was the same face and figure over and over again — but of course, these happenings were simply attributed to children's imagination and fantasies. As such, I never paid much attention to them, and eventually they ceased several years later.

Azi was a Boy Scout with his school's Boy Scouts Troop, and on one field trip during school holidays, he and his fellow Scouts were taken on a camping trip to a rubber estate in the Malay Peninsula. He outwardly displayed a sense of bravado and macho but deep inside, I expect he was none too keen about sleeping on the ground in a sleeping bag inside a canvas tent, without the privilege of servants at his beck and call. He also lacked a younger sibling upon whom he could take out his frustrations.

Mosquitoes were not a favourite of his either. And who would be serving him his daily meals? He did not even know how to boil an egg. Dad must have convinced Mum that this was a good training ground to prepare him for adulthood, and so she, too, after much punctilious deliberation, agreed he should participate in this field trip. He was away for about a week, during which time the rest of us at home had our own field day rummaging through his toys and reading his closely guarded comics without fear of being chased around the grounds and getting drenched by his water pistol, or getting a smack over the head, or bruised arms from his pummeling, or sore legs from being pelted with his toy gun that fired cork bullets.

On the first night of his return home, and as smell travels faster than sight and sound, he reeked of stale perspiration. He also complained of an intense headache, an unusual affliction for him. Ah Chwee immediately sent him for a hot bath, about which he complained incessantly. In the meantime, she prepared a poultice for his headache and made a hot chocolate for him before he was sent to bed. Mum looked curiously at Azi's face. In fact, I observed her gaze to be focused just about an inch above his head and not directly at his face. Her eyes appeared to be illuminated with a hint of moisture as they appeared glazed and distant. Those were not tears, I was sure of it. This made me even more curious as to what was wrong with my brother. What had my mother gleaned?

She then instructed Ah Chwee to place a cut lemon inside a jug of water and to place the vessel beside my sleeping brother during the night. Ah Chwee was also not to move the jug, touch it, or disturb its contents. This was a rather bizarre instruction, but Ah Chwee, whilst not understanding Mum's purpose, obeyed her 'Mem's' instructions without question.

The following day was a Thursday. I remember it well because on Thursdays at sundown, Dad ritually would light a small charcoal fire in a ceramic receptacle or brazier and burn small pieces of frankincense, which would sizzle over the red-hot coals in the brazier. He would then walk around the entire house and outside the verandah with the frankincense emanating through the air. The heady fragrance from the fumes was to be dispensed around the house and garden whilst he chanted prayers to invoke angels, good tidings, and blessings on the household. I overheard Ah Chwee reporting to Mum that during the entire night, Azi was mumbling in his sleep, and the stench of stale perspiration overwhelmingly permeated the room throughout the night, despite his having had a jolly good bath and scrub before bedtime. She also complained that, owing to all of this, she could not catch a wink of sleep. She also reported that the lemon-infused water in the jug had mysteriously turned black by the morning, and this had her quite spooked. Mum said nothing but just nodded and told Ah Chwee to throw the sullied water into a monsoon drain outside of our house and dispose of the jug into the garbage bin outside of the house. She was to exit the house through the back door and was strictly instructed not to bring the jug back into the house again. After the disposal,

Ah Chwee was to clean her hands with some soil first and then wash her hands at the tap outside the house in the courtyard — the same water outlet Moona used to wash our clothes.

Azi looked a bit strange that day; his eyes took on a dark beady appearance, and his pupils appeared to dilate, taking on a rather intense look, as Ah Chwee observed and reported to Mum. His usually neatly combed hair with a side parting was dishevelled — practically standing on end. Ah Chwee just thought that he was malnourished through a lack of good food during the camping trip and succumbed to some sickness. Then at sundown, my father lit the frankincense burner and was proceeding to carry out his ritual by walking around the house with me in tow. You see, I was Dad's shadow whenever he was at home. Azi was on the verandah looking lethargic and was lounging on a wood-and-wicker planter's recliner chair, like an Australian blue-tongue lizard in repose. A planter's chair is a favourite item of rattan furniture usually found in rubber or oil palm plantation bungalows in Malaya. A fellow Freemason gave Dad one such chair, the Estate Manager for one of the Sime Darby rubber plantations stationed in the State of Johore. As soon as Dad, holding the incense burner and chanting the prayers, walked past Azi, he suddenly bolted up straight from his repose, and his eyes took on a really menacing look.

"Give me toh-ddy! I want toh-ddy!" he bellowed in a voice that was very many years older than that of an eleven-year-old boy. Toddy, a high-content alcoholic drink made from coconut sap, is frequently consumed by Indian rubber plantation labourers. "Yaaar... toh-ddy! Toh-ddy!" Azi shouted.

As I have mentioned several times, children generally know no fear. Despite this sudden physical change in my brother's voice, appearance, and behaviour, I casually walked up to him from behind where Dad was standing, still holding the incense burner.

I innocently said, "Azi, how come you look so funny?"

All hell broke loose at this point. Well, virtually. He suddenly sprang up from the recliner with amazing speed and force and lunged at me. He firmly grabbed my throat and pressed hard with his bare hands. Awfully hard.

"*Marrri sama saya! Marrri sama saya!*" he growled in Malay, commanding me to accompany him to the other parallel world, with a guttural emphasis on the 'r' sound of the word 'Mari', like as an Indian coolie would say it. Our childish skirmishes never involved actions as life-threatening as strangulation. The odd slipper or toy being hurled, a smack on the head, the use of water pistols, cork bullet guns and rubber band catapults, at worst, a blow to the upper arm were the usual forms of weaponry and attack. But now, his eight-year-old younger sister was being violently strangled, and there was no apparent sign of his letting go. Dad, about two feet away from this attempted murder, shouted at Azi to let go of me.

With an even more diabolical gleam in his eyes, he turned his head towards Dad and shouted, "*Mampus! Mampus sekali!*" Die! Die all together!

In the meantime, I was gagging. My tongue was slowly but surely endeavouring to make an outward appearance, and my eyeballs must have attempted to take leave of their sockets. As if by telepathy, Mum suddenly appeared out of the woodwork. She grabbed hold of Azi and, uttering some unfathomable words under her breath, started pummelling the boy with her fist. Then she and Azi, or what was supposed to be Azi, started a dialogue in a strange language, which I found out many years later, was the ancient mystical language called Pali.

The pummelling continued for a few more blows, and then her eyes darted towards Dad as she ordered him to hurl the hot coals at Azi. The tone of her voice clearly indicated that she was not joking, nor was there any room for debate. Realising what was happening and what Mum was doing, Dad hurled the entire brazier with the red-hot coals and the smouldering frankincense at Azi. He immediately fainted and invariably let go of my throat. Incredibly, there was not a single bruise on his body from Mum's pummelling, nor a single burn mark on his body from the hot coals! Mum continued to chant some more incantations, and finally, she called for a glass of water containing an immersed lime cut in half to be brought to her. She then chanted some final words into the glass and threw the water at her fallen son, who thereupon woke up with a jolt and started to cry.

Dad, meanwhile, carried my limp body into the house and cradled me in his arms until I stopped wheezing and the colour returned to my cheeks. By the time Merifa and Ah Chwee took over from my parents, both Azi and I were completely exhausted but somewhat adequately recovered to be taken away for a bath and some sustenance.

The following day and after all the commotion had completely died down, I heard Mum explaining to Dad that Azi had inadvertently become possessed by the spirit of an Indian rubber tapper labourer. This occurred whilst he was on the Scout camping expedition when he pitched his tent and slept under a particular rubber tree. This very same tree was the one where the labourer had hanged himself. She was told all this by the spirit of the Indian labourer during their dialogue exchange in Pali. The spirit had designs to take my brother and me with him to the other parallel world to be his companions. To achieve this, he would make Azi weaker each day from his sickness until the poor boy would succumb to it. Had I perished from the strangulation attempt, I would have joined the spirit first, ahead of my brother, Azi.

MY FATHER IS POLICE, LAH!

The day after this incident, and in the days, months and years that followed, Azi had absolutely no recollection of what had happened the previous two nights and still does not remember. When Mum was relating the incident to Dad the following day, Azi just stared confoundedly at her, wondering why she was fabricating this ridiculous story. Thereafter, if ever the subject was raised, he would laugh and say we were making it up just to make him appear silly. One did not have to make up anything to make him appear silly. He was. And arguably, still is.

At the time, I did not have any idea what Mum had done to remedy the situation nor how she instinctively knew what had occurred at the precise time. I could not fathom why she ordered my father to throw hot live coals at an eleven-year-old boy — his own son and heir no less -- and that Dad, without any hint of doubt or contradiction, did exactly as she bade.

It was years later that I discovered that Mum had a gift. She was born with the uncanny ability to be receptive and defensively react to negative supernatural forces, the same ability my older sister, to a greater degree, and I, to a lesser one, also possess. Mum used to tell me of spooky incidents when she was growing up in Ceylon. Of the eleven children, she appeared to have been chosen as the one to be born with an extraordinary gift of second sight. She used to see headless beings and other ghostly apparitions wandering about their huge bungalow in Kandy, Ceylon, which she reckons may have been negative energies of past lives, probably an accumulation of spirits of fallen soldiers or civilians during the two World Wars. My grandparents' house was a large old-fashioned colonial bungalow built during the Dutch occupation of Ceylon. The colonial British thereafter commandeered this bungalow, and my grandfather was allocated this property when he was assigned as a District Officer with the British Governor of Ceylon. The house and grounds were large enough to accommodate him, his wife, and eleven children, each with their own bedrooms, quarters for fifteen servants and their families and my grandfather's car and two private rickshaws, which were used to transport the servants and my grandmother around the picturesque town of Kandy. The most notable aspect of the house was a large subterranean storehouse. My grandfather was a very astute man with a keen sense of foresight. His remarkable and commendable foresight gave him the direction and inkling to amass and clandestinely store enough dried meat and produce to see him, his family, his servants, and their families substantially nourished over both World Wars. Whilst the less fortunate were consigned to eat banana stems and tapioca, my grandfather's household had the luxury of meat every day, which invariably was a scarcity during the war years.

These ghostly visions obviously used to make Mum extremely vulnerable to psychological trauma and sicknesses, and so my great aunt, who was my grandmother's youngest sister, took Mum to consult with a local shaman called a *maniyo* and sought to heal her of her affliction. Instead, the *maniyo* offered to extend to my mother schooling and training in the art of supernatural defences, which my great aunt, thankfully, decided was a good thing.

Therein rests the consequential evidence of Mum's adroitness in ghostbuster skills.

10

A Prophet's Consternation

July 21, 1964, was a day that many will remember, but not fondly. It was the day that Mr Peter Butterworth had warned Dad about. It was the day in 1964, as it was in previous years, that was marked in the colonial calendar as Prophet Mohammed's (PBUH) Birthday. As was the norm, Muslims would parade down the streets enclosing the Padang and proceed to Beach Road and Arab Street towards the suburb of Geylang, which was the predominately Muslim Malay quarter of Singapore. Both Mr Butterworth and Dad had been appointed Acting OCs of their separate Police Divisions following the swift departure of the serving OCs and the CP to their holiday bungalows in Malaya. Since their meeting at the Magnolia Milk Bar, Mr Butterworth had been transferred to the Beach Road Division Station.

The procession started off peaceably, and the Malays carrying their decorated staffs of *bunga manggur*, decorative staffs with long petals of brightly coloured tinsel wound around the ribs of coconut fronds, held high and chanting praises to their Prophet (PBUH). Both police officers, upon receiving a tip-off from the waitress Nancy, had already primed their troops to be at the ready in the unhoped-for event that something, anything, would spark off a racial commotion.

There are different accounts of how, why, and what happened to spark the riot. Some say that a few straggler Malays had broken away from the parameters of their lines and when requested by a Chinese policeman to get back into line, took offence and spurred the anger of other Malays by saying a Chinese policeman was bullying them. Another report said that a Chinese youth, perhaps it may well have been Nancy's boyfriend, hurled a broken bottle at the Malay crowd, sparking off a rampage of colossal magnitude. As the saying goes, a small leak can sink a great ship, and whatever the actual catalyst may have been caused the proverbial ship to take on tonnes of water faster than the *Titanic*.

Earlier, the then Malay Head of State of Singapore, the Yang di Pertua Negara, Mr Yusof bin Ishak, earlier in the afternoon, made a formal address to the Muslim Malays gathering. He urged them to follow the fundamentals of Islamic teachings of "patience, forbearance and industriousness". The message appeared not to have permeated the crowd. The riots were said to have started around 5:00 p.m. when the Malays, goaded by Chinese thugs hurling bottles and rocks at the procession, called upon the equivalent of ethnic Malay samurais to come forth and defend the group. These fighters, known for their Malay martial arts combat called bersilat, suddenly appeared in full costume and in full force. They were armed with long blade cleavers called parangs and traditional Malay curved daggers called krises and were poised for mortal combat upon command. In the meantime, the Chinese provocateurs had set about torching buildings, cars, and houses—indeed, anything that came within reach of their flaming torches. The situation was dauntingly hazardous, and the Police Riot Division and Reserve Units had to be mobilised to control the mounting insurrection. On the first day of the riots, twenty people were killed, and many others injured.

MY FATHER IS POLICE, LAH!

In an isolated incident, Dad was summoned to arrest a small group of mobsters who had congregated outside a small mosque in the district of Geylang. Equipping themselves with full riot gear, he and his band of policemen arrived at the scene, beating their truncheons on their riot shields as they drew towards the mob. At the same time, the Police Riot Squad quickly realised they were considerably outnumbered by the rioters, who were wielding broken bottles and bamboo poles– not quite a match for the short stumpy batons and shields of the policemen. But Dad had his revolver, as did the other police officers, and whatever was said and done, a loaded gun spoke louder than a bamboo pole.

Notwithstanding Dad's sudden burst of patriotic courage, as if by a Heaven-sent act of divine intervention, the Singapore Police Reserve Unit and a contingent of Gurkha troops arrived – a timely arrival of the cavalry to what otherwise could have turned into a bloodbath with Dad and his Police Riot Squad being at a gross disadvantage. Upon seeing the strength of the newly arrived armed defence force, the rioters quickly dispersed, abandoning their poles, broken bottles, and various articles of clothing scattered along the street. Once the melee had ended and every last rioter had dispersed, the door of the red Police Reserve Unit van was flung open, and a strapping British Officer stepped outside. Upon removing the metal air raid helmet and riot gear mask from his face, a shock of blonde hair broke loose and accompanied by a wave from a muscular arm, a handsome set of white teeth greeted Dad.

"I say, Tez!" came the familiar cry of a very welcome voice. It was none other than Detective Inspector Peter Butterworth, Acting OC from the Beach Road Police Station, leading the cavalry reinforcements to the rescue.

"I say, Peter!" came Dad's relieved reply. The two officers

exchanged salutes and shook hands. "I can't think of a better time to see your face, Peter. You're indeed a sight for sore eyes, old boy!" quipped Dad.

This riot was not dissimilar to a previous riot in December 1950, which was sparked off by an overwhelming overreaction by the Malay community towards the case of a young Dutch girl, Maria Hertogh. She was adopted and brought up by a local Malay woman and was going to be forcibly deported to Holland to be reunited against her will with her Dutch biological parents. In that riot, the odds grossly outweighed the advantages. Dad and his riot squad team of Muslim Malay constables confronted the group of more than two hundred outside the Cold Storage building on Orchard Road. I have always regarded my Dad as the wisest person ever, but what he did at that moment makes me wonder whether he could have let his astuteness take a short, well-earned holiday. With his baton arm raised, he shouted to the riot squad, "Charge!" and ran towards the mob. He took about ten paces forward and, to reassure himself of his backup, looked back and stopped short. The police constables had not moved forward and just stood still at a safe distance and watched as the mobsters started to close in on Dad, a lone police officer standing in the face of more than two hundred angry Muslim Malay rioters.

I remember when Dad recounted this incident to me; he said he was not sure which of the two parties looked the more puzzled—the rioters or himself. The police constables, mostly Muslim Malays, had loyalties split between support for their own community and neutrality as active sworn-in members of the Singapore Police Force to enforce the law against street violence, indeed, any form of anarchy. Invariably, in support of Maria Hertogh's foster mother, who was ethnically Malay, the policemen, as were the rioters, felt they had to stand up for and support their own ethnic group. Their beliefs would not have made them better persons; only their actions would.

Dad recalls, "Retreating would have been a fatal mistake but very likely the most instinctive move under the circumstances. But I was a police officer, not a mere constable. I recognised the covenant which I had sworn to the Force, to uphold and defend the Law with honesty and integrity."

> "The superior man thinks only of virtue; the common man thinks only of comfort." — Confucius

Dad, realising the precariousness of his position, momentarily did away with his 'discretion being the better part of valour' philosophy and reached down to his holster to draw his service revolver. As the mob moved in on him, Dad must have taken on his icy-cold hard glares, which was a sufficient warning signal to the rioters that he meant business. Some in the crowd ran away, but those who tried to test him found that this was no picnic in the park. Dad fired three warning shots in the air, and wonder of wonders, the crowd panicked at the sound of the gunshots and dispersed in all directions. As Dad recalls, "They were all cowards. I was prepared to die for my country."

Thank Heavens that did not happen. Failing which, Mum would have been made a young widow and, highly likely, married to someone else. Correspondingly, I would not have been privy to his account of this incident.

In the end, his courage and dedication to the Force earned him the unflinching respect of his peers and the public. The reality is that Dad's Guardian Angel was already used to clocking in overtime.

The Police Force with the assistance of the Malayan Federal Police Reserve and Riot units that were dispatched from across the Causeway were unable to quell the violence and disturbances of the Prophet Muhammed's (PBUH) Birthday racial clashes after two days. Inevitably, a nationwide curfew had to be declared. This was, of course, very welcome news for school children. Children know no fear. Those of us who were in semi-boarding schools were recalled home under police escort and those in full-time boarding schools with parents or guardians overseas remained in their dormitories under tight security. We were all commanded to stay indoors and only police personnel were permitted out on the streets on patrol duty.

The Singapore Government found that the Malay Regiment and the Federal Reserve Unit could not effectively enforce the curfew. As a result, the Gurkhas, renowned for their no-holds-barred bravery and impartiality -- were called upon to uphold the curfew and patrol the streets. Nationwide roadblocks were set up with barbed-wire barricades, particularly along the main downtown streets and the Muslim Malay quarters. When the curfew was lifted for a few hours, stranded people accommodated in temporary shelters could return home or gain access to the few operating grocery stores to buy provisions. The Gurkhas were out in all their might, armed with rifles and on full alert. They were ordered to shoot any curfew-breakers on sight, keeping potential troublemakers at bay.

Dad was on full duty, and Daeri had to be recalled to the Force to supplement the beat patrol policemen during the curfew. Mum was home with us, as all Government offices were closed during the curfew. She insisted our doors and windows be locked and barred to stop any straggler rioter who might try to force their way into our house, as ours was known as a police officer's residence. Her idea was not one of her usual bizarre panic-provoked schemes. We did have an occasion when an escaped prisoner from the nearby Outram Road Government

MY FATHER IS POLICE, LAH!

Prison ran through our garden with several prison wardens behind him. At the time, Kebun was trimming the hedges, so he too joined in the chase, still holding on to his pruning shears for added pageantry. On account of the warden's whistleblowing, shouting and ensuing general pandemonium, this also attracted the attention of Zubaidah who was in the master kitchen boiling a kettle of water. Upon seeing her husband in full flight, pruning shears and all, she too decided to join in and waddled behind, the kettle in hand. What did she intend to do with it? Enough said. The escaped convict managed to shinny up the jackfruit tree and leapt over the back fence, through the kindergarten premises and vanished from sight. When they reached the fence, both Kebun and Zubaidah decided to abandon the pursuit and leave the wardens to it. Apart from anything else, they were both out of breath having run fifty yards.

Mum bundled everyone, servants included, into the main house and told them to remain there until Dad returned from duty. When he did, there erupted a lot of commotion in the house, particularly from Mum. Dad entered the front door with his police tunic top severely bloodstained. Even with my naïve and childlike level of common sense at the age of eight years, I had the capacity to deduce that Dad was not limping or hobbling and, as such, determined that the blood could not have been his own. But Mum went into histrionics. She thought that Dad had been shot and wounded. He managed to quell her fears and calm her down a little, but she still regarded him with suspicion.

I was able to glean from eavesdropping on their conversation that Dad was on his way home from the Station after duty hours. While driving, he happened upon a melee a few blocks from our house. With his Guardian Angel clocking in O.T. yet again, and the 'discretion being the better part of valour' policy being tossed out of his car window, Dad stopped his car, got out and saw a gang of Chinese youths attacking a hapless motorcyclist, who as it turned out, was neither Malay nor Chinese. He was a Eurasian trying to return home after the curfew was lifted. The gang pounced on the poor chap, started walloping him with bamboo poles, and then set fire to his motorcycle for good measure.

Dad drew his revolver and fired a warning shot into the air, a polite invitation to the thugs to leave the scene. Dad then helped the injured man into the passenger seat of his car. Whilst driving him to the General Hospital, the victim fainted and slumped onto Dad's shoulder, hence the bloodied tunic. Dad must have had exorbitant Life Insurance premiums back then!

The Government arrested about three thousand people including six hundred secret society members and 256 people were charged with possession of dangerous weapons. The rest were arrested for violating the curfew. The curfew lasted for eleven days, during which time, we children were exempt from school. The irony of it all was that when we were at school, there were a hundred and one things that we could think of doing at home if we were on holiday. But during the curfew period, we never did any of them; the excitement of the situation was enough to keep us suitably occupied. There were some advantages, though – I, for one, became the household champion at the Malay game of Five Stones – a game similar to the game of Jacks, which uses five stones or if one were fortunate enough, the stones would take the form of five pieces of material sewn in the shape of small triangular sacks, filled with green beans. The game involved throwing one of the stones in the air whilst scooping one, two, three and then four of the remaining stones off the floor and catching the air-borne stone with the use of one hand only. I was told this game was reported to severely contribute to the gradual demise of one's handwriting, and hence the 'E' I would be awarded on my Report Card for 'Writing'. The 'E' would be written in red ink.

Several weeks after the curfew had been lifted and on another visit to the Magnolia Milk Bar, Mr Butterworth met Dad again to give him a heads-up on the latest bit of Forces gossip. He informed him that both OCs and the CP were given Early Retirement Notices by the British Colonial Governor for deserting their posts during a national crisis. Dad and Mr Butterworth, however, received Bravery Medals from the Yang Di Pertua Negara, and a promotion in rank with a corresponding wage increase. But the most disheartening news of all was that Nancy had not reported for work since the curfew had lifted and appeared to have gone missing.

We never saw her again at the Magnolia Milk Bar.

11

Extra-Curricular Activities

It was (and still is) essential that children from privileged households be well-versed in all sorts of extra-curricular activities. This was not predominantly done in aid of the child being well-versed with skills apart from the Three R's, but served to give their parents leverage over other parents and peers, as a measure of evaluating one's social status. Only the wealthy could afford to send their children for ballet, pianoforte and violin lessons, elocution coaching and other such activities in the 1950s and the 1960s. Netball practice, athletics, and swimming coaching did not count—because the schools provided this as part of the curriculum in any case.

Azi and I were sent for pianoforte music lessons; my first lesson was when I was six years old and Azi a year earlier. Our lessons were conducted by a woman who evidently hated children. Miss Floringale, as we were to address her, was the sort of person who children's books writers and their readers would best describe as an ogress or a beast. In those days, it was not criminal to beat children. This archaic rule has since been dispensed with, but in many instances, as seen by the antics of the current young generation, there are grounds for saying it ought to be brought back.

MY FATHER IS POLICE, LAH!

From what I understood through conversations between my parents and their friends, Miss Floringale was thought to be the equivalent of a failed novice nun of the Carmelite Order. Perhaps this woman did not regard it as ethnic or religious prejudice to beat her students to what seemed like within a frazzled inch of their lives with various implements, the worst being a thin wooden ruler smacked across our hands and fingers. On one occasion, I caught sight of the ruler steering towards my left hand and attempted to retract my hand to avoid the blow, only to catch the corner of the ruler which scraped across my hand. I still have the scar, albeit faint, on my left hand.

Corporal punishment could be accompanied by shouting right into our ears and then she had the gall to ask whether we were deaf when we could not hear we had played a wrong note. Tweaking the short hairs on the side of our faces and pulling our ears were also in her repertoire. On one occasion, she pulled so hard at Azi's ear that the skin behind his ear was slightly torn and drew a slight trickle of blood. This prompted my mother to immediately write to Miss Floringale, admonishing her. "Kindly refrain from pulling off my son's ears. They are the only pair he has," she wrote.

She never wrote to Miss Floringale about all the other forms of physical abuse. You see, Mum already was convinced of the merits of walloping us. This and other forms of physical and psychological torture were the order of the day during our pianoforte lessons. Indeed, it also was a partt of educating all children in that era.

The main point of contention and perplexity was and still is, why would my mother pay good money to this woman to physically abuse her own children when she herself possessed the full capacity and licence to beat us herself? And for free? She knew her children were being tortured once a week by this excuse of a music teacher, but her focus was on academic achievement, and the order of the day then was the idea of browbeating children into submission and obeisance.

"Send your children for piano lessons to Miss Floringale," she would boastfully announce to her friends and associates, "Guaranteed Pass (referring to the practical and theory Pianoforte Examinations), I guarantee you." That summed up totally what was expected of us -- we were sent for piano lessons to pass the annual Grades Examinations, not to develop a love and appreciation of music.

Now pause for a moment and imagine an eight-year-old going for a pianoforte practical examination. In the first instance, the Examinations held at the Petrof Piano Studios utilised a Petrof piano, which was quite a different instrument from the Challen piano at our home and at Miss Floringale's. All conventional pianos have the same number of keys, but not necessarily the same type of piano stools. The Petrof piano stool resembled a rather tall hump-backed turtle and I had to be lifted onto it by the Examiner after my two failed attempts to climb onto the piano stool. Then I hopelessly slid off again.

My first pianoforte Associated Board of the Royal School of Music (ABRSM) Examiner was a kindly English lady whose greying hair was tied up in a bun and she had thin wisps of hair cascading down the side of her face. She must have thought it amusing, or perhaps dare I say, cute watching this little child, dressed in a pink party frock, wearing frilly socks and pink shoes, and her long hair tied in a matching pink ribbon tied into a bow at the top of her head, trying to ascend Mount Piano Stool. Eventually, I made it onto the piano stool, but getting my feet to reach the piano pedals was another matter. My first attempt to reach down to the pedal resulted in my bottom sliding completely off the piano stool. My concentration and determination to complete the music piece were so intense, that I continued playing standing up until the end. The fact that I was awarded a Distinction by the Examiner that year, I surmise, would not have been related to the merit of my music performance but on the strength of my resolve and the entertainment value of watching an eight-year-old contemplating the mechanics associated with a piano stool and pedals!

We used to be driven to our music lessons by Daeri, with our *ayahs* in tow. On the days when Miss Floringale would fly off the handle at us, I would leave the premises tearful at the end of the lesson. I still hate that woman!

Azi would pull a brave face — he was a prince first, a male child second, and was thereby groomed to never stoop to shedding tears, particularly due to a preposterous woman like Miss Floringale. Our *ayahs* would try to console us, but it was Daeri, who would immediately get out of the car and rush towards me. He would then carry me, still sobbing inconsolably, to the car with one hand cradling my head to his shoulder. He always made it a point on Wednesdays to come prepared with two small bars of milk chocolate or chocolate wafers as consolation for the obviously excessive harassment.

There were, of course, the occasions when Miss Floringale would be satisfied with our performance if we adhered to her intense practice regime. I endeavoured to keep with this schedule of practising rigorously, but Azi being ever the vengeful hot-headed prince, had other ideas. He was determined to break this woman and devised a magnificent and devilish scheme by which he would accomplish this. This Snake Year child was going to put his best diabolical devices into action, and Miss Floringale was going down.

Music lessons fell on a Wednesday, and we children knew the meaning of being stressed out, with an overwhelming sensation of fear emerging a day or two before. Azi would not practice as much as he ought and to this end, he would threaten me with a buffet of physical abuses if I should rat on him and tell Miss Floringale that he had not practised. Inevitably, after the first fifteen minutes of playing all the wrong notes, she would realise that this boy had not touched the piano since his last lesson. This invariably meant that he received the teacher's expected berating and beating. When asked why he had not practised, he would reply with boyish innocence that he had. At this juncture, she would swing her focus onto me, sitting apprehensively outside the music room, awaiting my own punishment. My father always impressed upon me the importance of telling the truth, so I was in a dilemma of whether to tell on Azi and get clobbered later or tell a lie and betray my Dad's expectations. I took the Buddhist way out and did neither.

"Did your brother practice his piano pieces?" Miss Floringale would bark at me, her eyes wide open like a rabid mongrel's. I did not reply. I merely nodded my head slowly, thereby not telling any lies on the one hand and on the other hand, not snitching on Azi, who invariably would shoot me a menacing look. Not convinced, she would continue with the interrogation, "Are you sure?" Same response with the slow and sage nodding of the head. "How many hours a day did he practise?" Unfortunately for both Azi and me, out of sheer intimidation, I had not grasped the question and I continued to slowly nod my head up and down. Then she realised the ploy and glared at Azi, who in turn looked at me with the corners of his mouth turned down and rolled his eyes in resignation.

If Miss Floringale possessed even the minutest iota of humour, she would have seen the absurdity of my reaction. If she had been intelligent, she ought to have questioned the two *ayahs* instead of an eight-year-old under the threat of persecution from an older sibling. But she wasn't.

Azi endured her berating until Grade III, whereupon he managed a mere scrape-through Pass for his Royal School of Music Examination. This should not in any way be regarded as evidence of him being dim. Stubborn? Yes. Thick-skinned? A resounding yes. Devious? Absolutely. His diabolical plan was to simply humour Miss Floringale and give his practice sessions 50 percent of effort as he headed towards his Grade IV practical pianoforte Examination. Her assessment of his capability was satisfactory, and she deemed him ready and prepared to take the Examination.

When the Examination Results arrived, he had failed; miserably and purposefully. He made a right disgrace of his music teacher, who had never before produced a failure amongst her pupils. In doing so, he thereby overturned her previously unsullied record and clean reputation. This led an overly distraught Miss Floringale to telephone my mother and tell her, "I cannot teach your son any longer."

This gave Azi a huge moral victory and the immense satisfaction of having broken this atrociously tyrannical woman while also escaping her clutches. Mum asked Azi why he had purposely failed the Exam, and his reply, coming from an eleven year-old, amazed her: "Respect has to be earned, Mummy, not awarded freely nor dutifully given."

Unbeknownst to him at the time, this circumstance also became the game changer in his life, pushing his musical abilities to new heights. My mother located a real music educator, not a teacher, whom Azi looked up to and regarded as his mentor and musical icon. This gentleman did not insist upon a rigid practising regime but instead taught Azi how to appreciate music in all genres. After all, Azi already knew how to read music. Now, he was going to expand his musical accomplishments by putting theory into practice, and in more ways than just the classical style. This turned out to be his professional calling, and he pursued his musical prowess with an unrivalled passion. Several years down the road from this encounter, Azi was engaged as the resident pianist at one of Singapore's landmark hotels, and he played at many other prominent public venues.

Therein lies the validation and sense behind the adage, "When music and courtesy are better understood and appreciated, there will be no war."

I continued on with Miss Floringale until I fulfilled Mum's aspirations of being a Music graduate. This commitment arose more out of courage rather than dedication. I daresay that after withstanding another six years of tuition ranging from satisfactory sessions to torturous ones, it gave me tremendous endurance and resoluteness in handling other challenging situations in life. There are just two possible outcomes of being subject to a barbarous teacher every week for ten years; either one succumbs to the tyranny and becomes obsequious, or rises above the bitterness and develops into a fully fledged street-fighter — not one who picks fights, but one who puts up a good fight when confronted.

I suppose I ought to be expected to say that my music lessons were bad. No, they were not; they were terrible. Despite graduating with flying colours, I quite predictably and understandably developed a mild level of psychological trauma, and to this day, I hesitate with trepidation to play the piano for an audience — be it one person or more. The presence of someone standing near me or watching me whilst I play the piano gives me a horrific recollection of Miss Floringale standing beside me, wielding her dreaded ruler. It gives me the creeps. All that money spent on ten years of piano lessons has amounted to nothing.

Several years later, I happened to be on a flight whereupon I was coincidentally seated beside one of Miss Floringale's former pupils. After engaging in some small talk and then discovering that we had had the same music teacher, I asked this person whether her lessons were conducted in the same vein as those which Azi and I suffered. The reply came, coupled with a reaction of eyes wide open in abject horror, "She used to whack me across my face so hard, that I fell off the piano stool every time."

As far as I am aware, not one of Miss Floringale's pupils became a concert pianist or professional musician. That speaks volumes.

Mum is afraid of water, in large doses, that is. She cannot swim and never had any intention of learning. When she was a child in Ceylon, she went on a family outing to the seaside at Trincomalee, where my grandfather rented a chalet for the family and some servants. The elder of her two brothers persuaded her and two younger sisters to climb into a large round wooden crate, which he would then cast off from the beach, assuring them he would be holding on to the crate and guiding it as it floated across the sea, to just within a manageable distance from the shoreline. That was fine until he lost his footing several yards into the sea and slipped. As he went under, he thankfully let go of the wooden crate, failing which the three girls would have accompanied him underwater. However, in letting go of the wooden crate, it started to drift further away with the current, with three screaming, panic-stricken young girls drifting farther out to sea. The brother, however, was fine. He resurfaced and endeavoured to swim after the runaway, no, float away crate, but the current was strong and moved the box away faster than he could get to it. Unlike the Owl and the Pussycat, the sisters had not been equipped with honey or money - not even a spyglass nor a paddle; they had absolutely no control of their vessel. Fortunately, my grandfather had been a competitive, strong swimmer and had undergone an

Advance Level Lifeguard Course. My grandfather managed to swim out, reach the crate, and guide it back to shore. The girls were understandably petrified but safe. Of course, the brother received a stern tongue-lashing from his father, mother, and sisters; indeed, just about everyone who was with the party — including a few passersby. From that day hence, my mother was terrified of water. She made a vow then and there that if she should have her own children, they would be taught how to swim.

There are some parents who believe the best way to teach a child to swim is to toss them into a river, lake or swimming pool and let them get on with it. Fortunately, Mum did not share this view and instead, sent us for a formal swimming course with an instructor at a nearby public pool. The course was to run over two weeks, with a session every morning. There would be a test at the end of the course and successful learners would receive a Certificate of Achievement. So Daeri, who was trained to swim at the Police Training School, was nominated as our personal lifeguard. He had instructions to follow us around the pool wherever the instructor went and he should never be more than three feet away from us at any time.

Our first basic swim stroke was to learn the dog-paddle. Apart from the embarrassment of our homegrown lifeguard tailing us, whereas the other learners did not need or have one. Paddling furiously with one's head bobbing up and down did not cover much ground in the interim period and it took much kicking, paddling and gulping heavily chlorinated water to get across the breadth, not the length, of the pool. After a week of lessons, Azi caught a dreadful cold and had to give up the remainder of the course.

I, however, took to the water like a swan. Well, if the truth be told, more like a duck. After mastering the dog-paddle, I learnt to float on my back. The instructor explained that even a strong swimmer will get tired and should flip over and float.

"When that happens, all you need to do is to lie flat on your back floating on the water, to catch a breather," he explained.

These two swimming techniques made up the sum total of the Beginner's Swimming Course. During the Test, we had to dog-paddle across the pool and, upon command flip onto our backs and float, and again on another command, flip and continue the dog-paddle until we reached the other end of the pool. And that is how I received my Beginners Certificate of Achievement from the Yan Kit Swimming Pool Course.

Ballet school was quite another activity altogether. I started ballet lessons when I was getting on to my fourth birthday. My first ballet school was the Red Shoes School of Ballet on Orange Grove Road, whose principal, Miss C. Vine, struck me as an awe-inspiring ballerina. To this day, I still have not ascertained what the 'C; stood for. Miss Vine would wear a bright red pinafore-styled leotard to which a short, frilled skirt was attached. She would wear pink ballerina tights and a pair of red ballet shoes to complete her ensemble. In fact, to set an iconic illustration, Mum used this image of Miss Vine as a prototype when she ordered a birthday cake for my fifth birthday. On top was a porcelain ornament featuring a ballerina wearing a red tutu with a red feather-down skirt attached and a red pair of ballet shoes. She was in an *adáge* pose; I still keep this porcelain ornament as I am a real sentimentalist.

Ballet lessons at the Red Shoes School were a passport to creating lots of new friends outside of the boundaries of our kindergartens and school classrooms. This is how Mr Butterworth's daughter Patricia and I became ballet chums. The school was domiciled in a large Palladian-styled colonial bungalow, which also served as Dean's School, a kindergarten for preschool expatriate children or privileged local children. Azi went to Dean's School for his preschool education. The owner and principal of the kindergarten was Mrs Robertson, who was well acquainted with my parents. Mrs Robertson, by then a widow, lived alone and apparently with a frugal lifestyle as she elected to occupy the servants' quarters of the bungalow as her accommodation. Initially, Dad and Mum would call upon her for afternoon tea whilst waiting for me to conclude my ballet lesson. As my Ballet Grades advanced after participating in a sequence of formal Royal Academy of Dancing Ballet Examinations, my parent's visits to Mrs Robertson became fewer and farther between, as I would then be accompanied to my ballet lesson by my *ayah*, who would have to sit in an enclosed servants' waiting area pen, a small area cordoned off within the bungalow's porch. There were brightly coloured painted wooden benches designated for the pupil's *ayahs* in the waiting area. The bungalow itself was built upon an undulating, sloped landscape, a climb up the driveway to the main building and a slope at the back, with a descending staircase leading to the courtyard and the servants' quarters. The architect, therefore, saw an opportunity to construct the bungalow on solid concrete pillars thereby availing a basement area to the building and correspondingly, entailing a flight of concrete stairs up to the main level of the bungalow. The mid-section of this staircase was embellished with a flat concrete rail resting on a line of green glazed ceramic Oriental-style balustrades, which lent a rather majestic-look to the main entrance. Around the garden were several pergolas supporting trellises of striking violet morning glory creepers and bright pink Honolulu flower creepers, all maintained by Mrs Robertson's Indian gardener.

    The principal attraction of the garden was Mrs Robertson's pet peacock named Boris. We had a challenge to see who could get near enough to steal one of its prized tail feathers, and hopefully, without Mrs Robertson being aware of our despicable intentions. Boris was not the most congenial of fowls and we used all kinds of tactics to seize one or two of his sought-after plumes.

One day, Patty brought a poorly constructed peacock's 'head' fashioned with a blue-painted tennis ball stuck onto the handle of an old bamboo-framed tennis racket, also roughly painted in blue. Two round marbles almost resembling eyes were stuck onto each side of the tennis ball, and these were painted black. Patty had even taken the trouble to draw eyelashes on each 'eye' to make the fabrication more convincing, with a view to imitating a real peacock, or peahen, as was the intention here. The aim was to dupe Boris into believing the imposter to be an attractive peahen mate. I was nominated to hold up this excuse for a peahen and slowly strut towards Boris, imitating a peacock's syncopated movements to distract him. Meanwhile, Patty would sneak up from behind and relieve its derrière of a plume or two. As the art of mime was also in the ballet curriculum, I had no trouble devising the movements of a peacock, syncopated head movements, the strut, and all.

For the first few moments, the ploy seemed to be working, and Boris approached me with a noticeable mixture of suspicion and interest. More importantly, he fanned his tail fully to demonstrate his mating prowess and likelihood of siring robust chicks. Seizing the opportunity, Patty scurried around Boris's back to pull out a couple of plumes. On my part, being bent in half and slowly strutting, I suddenly developed an urgent need to relieve flatulence. My mum always remarked that I had a belly and a backside like bellows as my posterior let off a loud volley of gaseous outbursts. This startled Boris, making him realise a conspiracy was afoot, and seeing Boris stopping dead in his tracks, Patty scooted away from Boris's posterior.

Maybe peacocks do not suffer flatulence the way humans do, but Patty did not know which of the two had let rip. Boris pivoted his entire torso and let out a horrified shriek — whether a result of being startled or from the putrid smell of my flatulence attack, who knows? It is still an enigma as to who received the bigger shock — Boris, Patty, or me.

Mercifully and as if on a telepathic command, Patty and I ran in opposite directions to confuse Boris as to whom he should pursue. He took a few steps to the left, chasing after me and then stopped short to swap directions to the right and chase Patty. This sequence of pivoting continued once or twice more, by which time Patty and I were well out of his range. Boris then strutted off with his head held high, indicating aloofness to disguise his gullibility which nearly caused him to fall victim to a childish prank. When we finally caught our breath and were well out of Boris' line of fire, and Mrs Robertson's for that matter, Patty and I hurtled up the steps into the main hallway and broke into a fit of laughter, with me still holding onto to the dummy peahen's head, still intact.

"Was that you who farted?" Patty asked with a giggle.

"Uhmm," I hesitated, out of wretched humiliation. "It might have been Boris."

In time, I graduated from the Red Shoes School of Ballet and advanced to higher ballet institutes, first the Taylor Dance Studio and finally, the Singapore Ballet Academy. But neither Patty nor I ever managed to purloin a single peacock plume from Boris.

I recall one rather curious incident, which occurred during my time at the Red Shoes School of Ballet when I was waiting for Daeri to pick me up from class. It only crossed my mind as being harrowing when I recalled the incident in later years, very many years later. But at the time, I must admit to being extremely naïve about the whole thing. Usually, Daeri would have been ready and waiting before my lesson's conclusion, but for some reason, he was late. Merifa, my *ayah*, was unwell that day, so I was at the school alone. All the other pupils had already gone home, and I was alone in the *ayahs* enclosure waiting for Daeri. Feeling extremely bored, coupled with a good dose of impatience, I decided to go under the bungalow to the basement area where the kindergarten playground equipment was kept and amuse myself on the brightly painted wooden slide.

I started to ascend and descend the slide a few times and after about five minutes or so, Mrs Robertson's South Indian gardener appeared in the basement and stood by watching me climb up the steps and then slide down the chute.

It is relevant to point out at this juncture that our ballet tunic consisted of a single-piece short pinafore-styled tunic top which came down to just below the line of our ballet bloomers, and the bottom of the tunic was slit from the waist down to allow freedom of movement. The tunic was fastened at the waist with a fabric coloured belt, the varying colours depicting our respective Grade levels. We wore red ballet pumps together with socks. As elementary ballet pupils in a tropical climate without air-conditioning, ballet tights were not required to be worn, thereby exposing the dancer's bare legs from ankle to upper thigh.

The gardener was slowly edging closer to the Slide, and he thereupon proceeded to remove his grubby shirt, revealing his bare chest, with just his dark khaki shorts remaining. Children know no fear. I continued my ascent and descent on the slide, unaware of this person's possibly ill intentions. As he eventually sashayed up to and stood directly beside the slide, he grinned lasciviously at me and asked, "You waiting forrr you fatherrrr?" spoken with the usual guttural emphasis on the 'r' sound, as heard by Tamil-speaking South Indians.

I just nodded, indicating that I was not interested in engaging in personal chit-chat with this fellow.

"Wherrre you fatherrr worrrk?" he persisted, edging closer and closer to the edge of the slide until he was just an arm's length away from where I was soon to be perched on the top of the slide.

I hesitated to answer until I arrived at the top platform of the chute and then retorted loudly, "PO-LICE!" As I slid down the chute, I added, "My driver also Po-lice, okay?"

Although I was consciously unaware of the gardener's intentions, whether honourable or not, I guess my policeman's daughter instinct prompted me to issue a deterrent warning against any improper thoughts by the coolie. As soon as he heard the word 'police' twice, both he and his seedy grin abruptly left.

When Daeri finally arrived, I recounted the incident to him in the car as we drove away from the school. It appeared to have caused him great anxiety and apprehension as it made him pull over on the side of the road, turn the car around and head back to the school. He parked the car under the porch and gave me strict instructions to remain in the car, with the car doors locked, whilst he went to the back of the bungalow's servants' quarters to where Mrs Robertson lived. He returned several minutes later accompanied by Mrs Robertson but without the gardener, who, according to her, had already left the premises upon completing his gardening duties. As she approached the car window, she gently tapped on it, and I wound down the window glass.

"Are you all right, dear?" she asked with a perturbed but kindly look upon her face.

"Yes, thank you, Mrs Robertson. Why?"

She did not answer my question and just said, "Not to worry, you're in good hands, Dear," and with that, nodded to Daeri and walked off. Daeri also did not shed much light on the foundations of this anxiety — perhaps he reckoned I had not quite come of age to be acquainted with such indecent matters.

The following week, when I went to my ballet class, a new gardener was on duty. He was Malay and looked to be about in our Kebun's age group. Daeri obviously relayed the incident to Dad, who discussed the matter with Mrs Robertson. Daeri also made absolutely sure that I fully understood his instruction that if I was left alone at the school and for any unforeseen circumstances he should be late again, I was to wait at Mrs Robertson's quarters. Dad, however, took it one step further and overruled Daeri's instructions — he gave a strict directive to Merifa and Daeri that I should never be sent to the Red School Shoes of Ballet unaccompanied again. Ever.

And he meant business.

12

HOUSE GUESTS

Visitors came and visitors left. This was generally the case except for one permanent house guest. My mother's youngest brother, known to us as Uncle Jack, came to Singapore and stayed at our house for the better part of four years whilst he trained with the British Royal Air Force at what was then the Seletar Air Base.

The larger of two storerooms in the main part of the house was converted into another bedroom and all the contents of that storeroom were relocated to the smaller one, making it virtually impossible to find anything without first taking half the contents out of the room. This house guest was of a rare breed in the category of lodgers; his understanding of the rules governing a guest was that they had the authority to help themselves to any and all of the domestic privileges availed in the household. It didn't matter to him that there was already a pre-set timetable and schedule formality, of servants' duties, household amenities and comestibles. He endeavoured to take over the management of the kitchen and to this end, it would not take a lot of imagination to visualise how the indomitable Zubaidah would react to this usurper. After several failed attempts to take control and despite being very much taller, stronger, and more ferocious looking than she, Zubaidah put up an admirable fight every time he endeavoured to boss her about. In the end, he yielded to Zubaidah's domestic superiority so as not to encourage a brisk termination of his freeloading of meals and the risk of having undetectable entomological titbits derived from the excretory systems of squashed insects dropped into his food. Uncle Jack conceded defeat.

I did not like Uncle Jack at all. Although he cut a very handsome and dapper figure, he was not of the variety of jovial, playful, and friendly uncles that one generally reads about in children's books. Perhaps he, too, hated children. The last thing we needed was a Miss Floringale duplicate hovering around us, especially a live-in variety. There never, not seldom, were occasions when he would return home from the Air Base bearing treats or gifts for the children, not to mention replenishing Dad's supply of beer, liquor, and cigarettes to which he regularly freely helped himself when at home. He was usually sullen with a disagreeable demeanour during most, if not all, of our waking hours. Thankfully, he only spent the minimum amount of time at home every month as he was generally stationed at the Royal Air Force Seletar Hills Air Base. I can only assume two reasons why Uncle Jack was such a miserable specimen; firstly, he was an unmarried Scrooge. Secondly, he was the younger of my grandparent's two sons, thereby denied any claim to be the heir; he was obliged to always remain in the shadow of his older brother, our Uncle Sunny, whose name and disposition were happily an exact match.

Mum did very little, if nothing, to get Uncle Jack to conform to the household arrangements and residence's matter of form. Most of all, she hardly considered it necessary to remind him that Dad's alcoholic beverages and supply of cigarettes would not automatically multiply or replenish themselves after Uncle Jack had consumed them, often leaving hardly a drop of liquor nor a cigarette left in my Dad's cache for his own enjoyment. This is just a little bit of evidence of my mother's propensity to overly favour the people from the family she was born into, rather than those from the family she created. Had it been Dad or me who behaved similarly — not that there would be even the remotest possibility — she would have been swift to reprimand and reproach us as guttersnipes and freeloaders. Or indeed, they would have suggested an ill-mannered casual visitor of similar demeanour and attitude would have to vacate the guest room P.D.Q. as a close relative was to arrive shortly, the room was required right away.

One of Uncle Jack's most annoying habits was to *hawk* excruciatingly loudly and then spit out of his bedroom window. Thankfully, his lodgings were on the ground floor of our bungalow, otherwise, the projectile could well have landed on an unsuspecting Kebun's head, or on any one of us if we happened to be in the garden near his bedroom window. It made me wonder how many of our unsuspecting cats might have been bombed by his missiles.

It was blindingly clear that Uncle Jack had not had the privilege of being acquainted with either *Miss Manners Guide to Excruciating Good Manners* or *De Brett's Guide to Etiquette and Modern Manners*. It would therefore be an extreme contradiction to use words 'Uncle Jack' and 'good manners' in the same sentence.

Azi had acquired and honed a self-taught obnoxious skill of letting off gas from either end, upon command. His skills of flatulence could be demonstrated at will; mine, however, was purely accidental. So, if he happened to be around when Uncle Jack let loose one of his disgusting phlegm-laden *'hawks'*, Azi would rebut this with a hefty outburst of gas from one end of his body or the other. By the time Uncle Jack had the time to swing around to identify and then admonish the miscreant, Azi would be well out of his visual range and in most cases, leaving behind a putrid odour for Uncle Jack's general edification and delight.

Such occasions inevitably led to Uncle Jack hurling a barrage of profanities at the unknown and unseen miscreant from his bedroom window. We had no idea what his phrases meant, but it all sounded fascinating to a brood of impressionable youngsters. My parents can therefore thank this unethical house guest for steadily introducing the household's children to unimaginably vulgar cursing.

Daeri did not like him either. Uncle Jack often commandeered Daeri to transport him to and from the Seletar Air Base, which was about twenty-two miles (32km) as the crow flies, from our house. He did this whenever he needed to report in at the Base. This, of course, would often conflict with Daeri's normal duties. Could this have been the reason Daeri was late picking me up that day from Ballet School when I encountered the gardener in the basement play area? Uncle Jack also had the gall to consider Daeri his personal batman as well, and he once tried to order Daeri to polish his military boots and tunic buttons. Daeri courteously but firmly declined, with the appropriate reminder that he was seconded from the Police Force and not the Army, to serve as Dad's exclusive Police batman. Thus, such orders could not be flouted unless express permission was first obtained from his Police Commanding Officer, that is Dad. Perish the thought that Dad was ever going to share this privilege with his freeloading, irascible, callous brother-in-law who had not achieved the appropriate rank to warrant his own batman from the Air Force.

Uncle Jack often argued with my *ayah* Merifa if she neglected to iron his tunic and clothes to his satisfaction. This was neither her paid assignment nor her responsibility in any case. I, however, *was* her responsibility. I vividly recall an occasion when I wanted a glass of milk which had to be made using milk powder briskly stirred into boiled water. Being absolutely disallowed to go anywhere near a hot stove for any reason whatsoever, let alone to boil water, I could not prepare a milk drink independently. I saw Uncle Jack standing at our front door and talking rather brusquely to Merifa shortly before leaving for the Air Base. I went up to Merifa and stood beside her quietly. When availed of a pause in the conversation, I made a polite interjection and asked her if she could please make a glass of milk for me. Uncle Jack glowered, and he bent down to face me eye-to-eye, his eyes opened wide with fearsome, manic aggression.

"Leave her alone, will you! What's the matter with you?" he barked straight into my face as droplets of saliva spurted from his mouth.

Had I been older, I would have put this down to this uncle possibly going rabid. Even Merifa was shocked. She was considerably shorter than he, but she heaved herself up to her fullest 5 feet 3 inches height and hissed at him, "Don't you DARE ever talk to this child like that again. If you are angry, shout at me. This girl is only eight years old. Shame on you!"

This outburst was just a prelude of more to follow, quite out of character for Merifa. She continued her criticism and scolding for his unacceptable behaviour as an uncle, my Mum's sibling, and my Dad's brother-in-law. She added, for good measure, that neither she nor any of the other household staff received a single cent in remuneration from him for their efforts in favouring, not serving, him with domestic tasks performed. As such, he had the lowest station and priority amongst the household staff and Dad's immediate family.

At that precise moment, Merifa's governess capacity took on a whole new meaning. Had she the entire household staff and not just an eight-year-old child as an audience, she would have received an overwhelming round of applause, a standing ovation for such a bold and powerful performance. Zubaidah herself would have danced one of her spirited jigs in celebration and baked a large *kueh lapis*, a local spiced cake consisting of a number of thin layers, just for the occasion.

I still wonder whether Merifa's defiance, her brutal verbal attack on his bullying tactics, and her fearless reaction humbled Uncle Jack. But without another word, he turned on his heels and walked out of the house to the main road to hail a taxi, much to the waiting Daeri's welcome surprise. Thereafter and whenever he was at home, he made a concerted effort to stay well out of Merifa's way and would even get up and move elsewhere if she happened to walk past. Shortly before Uncle Jack moved out of our house, much to Dad's, the servants, Azi's and my relief, he announced that he would be returning to the UK to marry his English girlfriend, who happened to be his housekeeper's daughter. As far as we were concerned, he could marry Rumpelstiltskin's daughter, we could not care less. A year later, he returned to Singapore with his English wife Susanna; herself a bit of a mousy-looking pale-faced English girl from Darlington County, Durham, whose outer appearance did, in fact, belie her true 'dragon lady' disposition. They set up home in the married quarters of the Seletar Air Base. Marriage and married life seemed to have calmed his temperament, particularly when he became a father of two. I am sure he would not have dared yell at his children if they wanted to ask for a glass of milk; Susanna would have bitten off his head.

My parents also entertained casual house guests, mostly visitors passing through Singapore from Ceylon or the UK. Those who arrived from Ceylon would generally be observed to leave our house with more suitcases than they had originally brought. Mum enacted specific house-guest legislation: whoever was visiting from Ceylon and hoped to stay with us was obliged to return to Ceylon with additional luggage of old clothes and toys to be distributed amongst Mum's sisters and their families. This would be clearly specified and in writing in the reply to the acceptance letter sent to the would-be visitors in response to the request letter received.

This was yet another avenue in which we were unwittingly and unknowingly relieved of our personal goods and chattels. Sent to my mother's sisters in Ceylon were all of my birthday frocks—some only worn once; my very first pair of red ballet shoes; my silvery white ballet tutu, which was specifically tailored for me when I was selected by the Taylor Dance Studio for a solo performance; another ballet costume for me as Sleeping Beauty when she climbs the stairs to reach the spindle and prick her finger; my first ballet *pointe* shoes and other collectables. I could have handed these down to my own children and likewise they to theirs, and future generations. I expect I suffered the psychological trauma of having my possessions violated, to the point of not wanting to establish contact with nor recognise any of those visitors for years. I could have shaken hands with them at a party and not known I was related to them.

Owing to the number of siblings Mum had, this entailed that each one of them would beget offspring at some point or other, and we would be inheriting a full battalion of cousins, once, twice, and thrice removed possibly, and Mum would have acquired the same number of nieces and nephews. When you happen to be fortuitous and have privileges, it is not any wonder how many unknown and distant relatives can suddenly sprout from out of the woodwork; so many that even if we were to trip and fall over them on a busy street, we would not know that we were related!

MY FATHER IS POLICE, LAH!

For the better part of our childhood years, Mum never failed to send our stuff to her siblings' families, thinking this ought to bedeck her from head to toe with eternal gratitude, a sense of power over her siblings and their children, unfailing loyalty and devotion and a barrel of praise for her generosity and thoughtfulness. If she was truly expecting all of the above from her kin, she was standing in the wrong queue when they were handing out relatives. Not only did her siblings complain, but also fought amongst themselves as to who should receive what — and when it dawned upon them that a settlement could not be reached, they complained to Mum, asking why she had only sent one of that specific item and not two, or more! I did witness the bickering on a few occasions. Not a single cousin thanked us for the clothes and toys they received. They assumed this was their entitlement until I put them straight in later years. I carried a lot of accumulated disdain for having lost all my precious toys and possessions to them — of course, I could not blame them for the loss as it was my Mum who unilaterally decided to give these away. By their receiving several new party frocks, boys' clothes, or toys, we, on the other side of the proverbial coin, were invariably obliged to lose the same and of a similar number, usually without our knowledge.

At least the items donated to the Children's Home went to children who were profoundly grateful. They would make *papier mâché* objects, cut-out pictures to make cards, D.I.Y. posters and what-not and send these to us every Christmas with a handwritten message of gratitude.

Dad played a prominent role within a local religious association, which was another one of his charitable activities. The association once decided to invite a renowned priest from Kerala, India, to come to Singapore and Dad offered to take responsibility for the priest and offer him free board and lodging at our house, while he applied for a full-time Residency Permit for the priest. We were introduced to this revered priest and were told to address him as *Moulana*; a form of address given to a Muslim scholar or Sufi mystic.

Moulana arrived shortly after Uncle Jack left for the UK, otherwise, one of the servants would have to share accommodation with another. Comparing the characters of Uncle Jack and Moulana was like comparing chalk and cheese. Uncle Jack was like an overbearing grizzly bear nursing a migraine, whereas Moulana was a spring lamb, a totally endearing man, soft-spoken and kind. Unlike our previous experiences with certain people mentioned earlier, this priest loved children. So, it came as no wonder that we and the servants' children, always found ourselves casually dropping in on him, and our visits were always made even more attractive when we received some trinket from him; a string of prayer beads, a coin or two, a miniature bottle of pure rose essence perfume, or some such, and all of these accompanied by a warm congenial smile. He had a gorgeous set of straight teeth, which availed him the most disarming smile. He was totally bald; but the complete loss of hair on his head was ably compensated by his luscious black curly beard, moustache and the hair on his chest and his back. If indeed he was to be given a bottle a shampoo, it would be intended for his face and body, not his head. Discounting the beard and moustache, his and Kebun's pates made a right pair.

Moulana was a large-built man with a very wide girth. You would have to have arms like an orang-utan to put your arms around his waist. He was also exceedingly kind to all the servants. As he was knowledgeable in religious texts and doctrines, he was never without the company of someone from our household, eager to discuss with him or simply listen to his advice and counsel. He loved his food — hence the wide girth. As he also endeared himself to the dreaded Zubaidah, she made a conscious effort to cook tasty premium-grade food for him as and when he needed nourishment, including puddings and cakes, which Moulana happily wolfed down. So now we knew he also had a sweet tooth.

The servants had absolutely no qualms about fetching and carrying for him, as they appeared to feel that offering their servitude also earned them his choicest blessings. Moulana, although a scholar of the Islamic denomination, was more evolved spiritually than religiously — he was probably what one would regard as a mystic. During the times I spent with him, sitting at his feet and listening to his stories, he used to show me a photograph album containing scores of snapshots taken during some of his very intense spiritual group assemblies. He would lead the recitation of verses and chants by the congregated followers to invoke such a frenzied atmosphere that the presumed power of a Pentecostal-like spirituality would descend upon the gathering and empower Moulana to perform some rather bizarre 'miracles'.

One of the photographs showed him holding two thin short swords, like stiletto daggers, poking into the eyes of a volunteer from the assembled congregation without causing a single drop of blood to fall, or worse still, rendering the volunteer blind. Another one depicted Moulana raising a paralysed man up from a wheelchair to walk again. Another showed Moulana with a chalice of burning frankincense whereupon the smoke emitted took the distinct form of a kris dagger. Moulana spoke of how he had completely healed a young boy suffering from epileptic fits, something that baffled doctors treating the child, and how he had the power to cure people afflicted by evil spirits and possessed by demons. I found this totally plausible—people being afflicted by demoniac possession—on account of a paranormal incident with Azi.

His power and ability were further endorsed when a young couple called at our house to seek Moulana's help. They brought their young sickly-looking daughter whose pallor was not far off that of cloudy dishwater. She looked my age but lacked my spritely and energetic disposition.

Moulana took one look at the poor girl and without requiring the parents to provide a diagnosis, he immediately instructed the servants to bring some flowers from our garden—seven different colours of seven different species—my Dad's charcoal incense brazier with the frankincense chips, some other household comestibles like limes, salt, rosewater, turmeric, and other mundane ingredients. He also asked for an empty glass bottle with a tight lid. With all his required implements and ingredients in place, he then changed into his special religious garb and instructed the *ayahs* and the female servants to keep themselves and the children well away from the back door of our house, which was where he was going to perform the ritual. The back door led to the courtyard connecting the main house to the master kitchen, which was Zubaidah's territory. Being very curious renegade children following our incorrigible leader Azi, upon his direction, we stealthily crept out in single file and escape the confines of our cordoned-off area. We exited from the house through the front door, went straight to the servants' quarters at the back of the compound, where we were then able to persuade Zubaidah, who herself was a champion of *Kay Pohs*, not dissimilar to the substantial Mrs Long, to allow us to watch from the master kitchen windows. And what a grandstand view that was! Moulana only permitted the younger male servants to assist him. Therefore, Kebun and the womenfolk were banned, but his son Jaafar, Zainal the sous chef, and Harris the shop steward, were called in as the backup brigade.

Moulana first instructed Jaafar to light a wood fire a short distance away from the courtyard. We then observed Harris carrying a dining room chair which he placed in front of Moulana. Once the fire was ignited and burning at full strength, Moulana asked for the girl to be brought to him. Her father carried her and carefully seated her on the chair. She sat down with her head bowed and tilted to one side, her arms dangling to her side. Moulana then ignited the frankincense chips and as the smoke arose, he started to invoke the name of God and recite religious texts and verses. He then took what looked like a piece of turmeric and cut lime and rubbed it on the girl's forehead, still chanting the prayers. The girl's head suddenly bolted up. Her body started to heave, and she appeared to take on a mysterious force of energy and she started talking in gibberish and in a male voice. Suddenly she leapt out of the chair and 'flew' towards Moulana who, anticipating this reaction, swung his arm towards the direction of the approaching airborne child and sent her hurtling a few feet back, landing with an almighty thud on the cement floor. Moulana continued with his prayers, and the girl suddenly picked herself up from the cement floor, as if she had simply fallen onto a bale of cotton wool and screeching, her voice now taking on that of a female banshee, again 'flew' a second time towards Moulana, who was poised and ready for this next onslaught. This, of course, demonstrated she was afflicted by more than one entity. Moulana caught hold of the girl, who was now suspended in mid-air as she had levitated to the height of his shoulder. She emitted saliva foam. To force her down into the chair, he summoned Jaafar, Zainal and Harris to come forward and pull her down. Of course, despite being full-bodied men, these three youths also happened to be the biggest cowards in the household. Their obvious hesitation to come forward signalled a need to recruit other cavalry to the rescue—none other than the indomitable Zubaidah and the rotund but sanctimonious Ah Chwee, who rushed out from the master kitchen to aid Moulana without any need to be asked first.

Seeing Zubaidah and Ah Chwee come forth gave the three chicken-hearted youths a rush of bravery, which induced them to come forward and redeem themselves from their initial faint-heartedness. Six adults, including her own father, tried to hold down the girl, but she appeared to be possessed of the strength of ten men. However, Moulana's chanting weakened her resistance, and eventually she was forced back into the chair with her head flailing from one side to another. From where we were crouched at the master kitchen window, this hindered our direct view of the full goings-on. We were all very silent, not daring to utter a single word as the whole incident was evidently taking its toll on our psyche.

Finally, Moulana asked for the glass bottle to be brought forward, and he opened the lid. With one hand holding the bottle and the other placed on top of the girl's head, Moulana chanted something and then appeared to slowly raise his hand off the girl's head, apparently clutching something invisible. This invisible entity he quickly put into the opened bottle and then immediately shut its lid. He then let go of the girl, who thereafter slumped into the chair but was quickly cushioned and lifted up by her father, who lovingly cradled her. Moulana held the bottle upright, flat upon the generous span of his palm. To our astonishment, the bottle started to wobble and gyrate. He then walked briskly to the blazing open wood fire and hurled the bottle into its flames. Miraculously, the bottle did not explode, but the wobbling and gyrating ceased immediately. This final stage of action brought the theatrical drama to a close. Moulana then told Zubaidah and Ah Chwee to prepare a hot water bath infused with the seven flowers, limes, turmeric, and rosewater ingredients. The servants put the ingredients in Moona's tin washing tub, which was used as a bathtub for the girl. With her clothes still on, Moulana immersed the now slightly recovered girl into the water and, whilst chanting more prayers, ladled the bath water over her head and torso. He then went indoors with instructions to the servants to prepare some dry clothes for the girl and toss her old wet clothes into the still blazing wood fire. Strangely, the damp clothes did not douse the flames of the fire at all.

The following day, when I was having one of my usual chit-chat sessions with Moulana, I asked him what and why all those things happened. He smiled wryly at me and asked, "Who asked you to disobey my instructions and watch all that?"

"Azi," I replied truthfully.

Moulana let out a hearty chuckle and shook his head. He then related this explicit account of the girl's affliction. In disobeying the laws of God and her parents' advice, the girl clandestinely entered the *kampong* house of a neighbourhood Malay shaman or witch doctor, known as a *'bomoh'*, out of sheer curiosity. Upon happening upon the *bomoh's* mystical taboo articles and implements, she started to dabble and play with them, without having the slightest notion of the danger with which she was dabbling. Upon being caught red-handed, the *bomoh* flew into a rage. Upon seeing the girl on her premises and having her privacy violated, she cast a spell upon the child by inflicting two of her kept *spirit conduits* to persecute and torment the child. This explanation drew a look of anxiety upon my face; Moulana was quick to notice my discomfort.

"My child," he said, "God is Great. Always remember this.

If God is always in your heart, no harm will ever come to you. I promise you."

I have never forgotten those words, that incident, or Moulana.

13

OF FRIENDSHIPS MADE AND PLEASURES SHARED

"The difference between school and life? In school, you're taught a lesson and then given a test; in life, you're given a test that teaches you a lesson"
— Lehte -

I was sent to an exclusive Methodist Mission School on top of a hill in a quiet and scenic part of Singapore. Beside the school was a famous luxury hotel that often hosted celebrities and movie stars from neighbouring Asian cities. Downhill and below the hotel was a popular cinema bearing the same name as the hotel. The Methodist Church's Bishop's Residence, a beautiful colonial bungalow with a gorgeous, manicured flower garden, was beside this hotel; the two buildings being separated by a flight of steps, known casually as 'the 100 Steps'. Actually, I had taken the trouble to count the steps ascending and descending them several times over; there were only ninety-seven of them.

The school consisted of a few quaint buildings scattered around the entire compound. These buildings surrounded a small playing field with only room for two netball courts and a bit extra. But in any case, it contained sufficient space to hold the annual Schools Sports Days. This event was comprised of relay team games and activities using quoits, rattan hoops, netballs, and bean bags. A large wood and canvas tent would be erected and decorated with colourful buntings to accommodate the prize table and seating for the visiting school dignitaries and the participants' (hopeful) parents. Each of the four individual school buildings was visually charming in architecture, being built by colonial architects with a flair for aesthetic artistry and practicality, as compared with the box-like concrete architectural disasters of modern-designed school buildings. The latter indicate financial aptitude, coupled with a disagreeable look, taste not having been a moral concern at the design stage.

My first, second, and third-year primary classrooms were in a double-storey elongated white building, which can be correlated in shape with a brick-and-mortar version of a Sarawak Iban Longhouse with a sloping deep-red tiled roof. The light green windows were fitted with pivoting large wooden panels that swung open and shut as required. Along the upper floor was a corridor enveloped by a wall barrier made of concrete and supported by glazed ceramic green balustrades at equidistant intervals. One side of the building at the ground floor level led to a grassy enclosure equipped with children's swings, a see-saw, and a brightly coloured jungle gym or monkey bars made out of reinforced steel tubes inter-connected with one another to form a rectangular steel framework structure. The other side of the building consisted of a walkway which connected to a flight of steps down to the school lavatories and further along the way to the School's Tuck-Shop, and Dining Hall for the boarding students.

Many of the children I became acquainted with during my kindergarten days also attended the same school. This was indeed a huge bonus as it meant not having to start from scratch to make new friends. Our teachers were encouraged to make regular contact with parents if any child behaved abominably or was a slow learner. I was definitely more of the latter. My initial School Reports lacked brilliance, and this mandated the illuminatory phone call to my parents, saying their child was not showing much academic prowess in becoming a bright crayon in the box, so to speak. Azi, who initially also suffered the same situation from his teachers, devised another one of his cunning plans.

He knew that as my parents' office telephone numbers could not be divulged for security reasons, given Dad's rank and position in the police, the teachers could only telephone my parents at home. With this in mind, he devised how we should intercept these incoming phone calls, presumably expected from our teachers, if we sensed they were on the verge of making contact to complain about us. Obviously, a teacher would have to obtain the home telephone number from us first during school hours, which indubitably heralded an impending phone call to the parents.

These teachers were not about to keep an organised record of each of the forty or so classroom students' telephone numbers, multiplied by three categories of classes in each age group, in a little black book, were they?

So on days when we expected these calls, we would be poised and hovering around the telephone desk to ensure that we would get to the telephone before anyone else. We already had become familiar with the voices of our own classmates and my parent's friends if they were to telephone. After all, a child's voice answering the phone would immediately signify that either Azi or I had answered. But here was the cunning part—a teacher would not know how many children or adults existed in our household. So, when the telephone is answered with the conventional "Hello", their usual first words would be "Who is this?" or "Who's speaking?"

How on earth did these imbeciles become teachers when they could not even deploy basic telephone manners to say, "Hello, may I speak with so-and-so, please? This is so-and-so calling here."

So, whenever we were got such a caller asking, "Who is this?" we would activate our counterattack with the reply: "*Hantu! 'Nak ikut 'tak'?*" followed by a diabolical laugh, like a ghost inviting the caller to accompany it to the netherworld. Usually, the caller would hang up before we did, stupidly thinking they had got the wrong number...or did a ghost channel itself through the telephone? A few seconds later, the telephone would ring again, perhaps the same caller trying again, out of bravery or stupidity or a combination of the two. We would then blow a shrill policeman's whistle down the phone as soon as we lifted the receiver, even before answering with a "Hello". Some diehard types would make a third attempt—this was not often, but it did occur once in a while. Azi would then simply lift the receiver, let out his signature resounding belch, "*BURRRRP*" and hang up. It was not often that our teachers sought to contact my parents by telephone, and is it any wonder?

Thereafter they wrote letters instead, which we had to return the following day, with the letter signed, endorsed, and dated by one of our parents. Azi had no difficulty forging Mum's signature and, for the princely sum of five cents, could sign my letter, too. We were never found out until the Report Cards arrived. Mum believed us otherwise to be fine examples of well-behaved and academically gifted model schoolchildren. We could evade presenting teachers' random letters to our parents, but not the end-of-term Report Cards.

While not having brilliant academic aptitude, I was quite popular at school based only upon the many plastic game tokens of *kuti-kuti* I had accumulated. I was a wizard at this game owing to adroitness with my fingers. My initial capital stock of one small cellophane packet of eight pieces soon propagated into an entire shortbread biscuit tin full of them within a year. The more my competitors lost their *kuti-kuti* to me, the more they would go out and purchase additional packets to repeat the challenge. This is how I earned my hard-sought reputation of being the *kuti-kuti* champion of my primary school. Several times, my opponents would lose all their *kuti-kuti* to me. Their sorrowful and despondent looks thereafter tugged at my heartstrings, and I would feel compassionate towards the loser and let them take a few pieces from my massive collection, free of charge, no provisos attached. These acts of kindness were mainly what made me appear not only as a daunting *kuti-kuti* challenger but also a popular classmate. As I was more skilled at *kuti-kuti* than Azi, my collection gave me a powerful bargaining commodity when I needed something from him or, correspondingly, he from me. To this end, I had struck an invaluable and profitable balance.

It had been drizzling the whole morning on that day. The afternoon was sticky with humidity as we were having a history lesson in our Primary Three classroom. There had been a few low rumblings of thunder earlier, sounding like a dog growling at another dog, before embarking upon mortal combat for a contested bone.

In the midst of being introduced to the Legend of Romulus and Remus during a history lesson, there occurred an almighty blast outdoors, which caused all the students and the teacher to cry out in astonishment. That was the loudest blast of thunder I had ever heard. The teacher stood still for a moment, the sudden blast clearly had shaken her. After regaining some level of composure, she endeavoured to keep the chattering students quiet and calm and then continued with the lesson. About fifteen minutes later, the school principal interrupted all activities with an urgent announcement over the P.A. system. All day school students should leave the school because the area and the roads surrounding the school were being cordoned off by Police roadblocks. We were not told what had happen, nor why we were to leave, but it was not difficult to attribute this sudden call of action to the earlier loud roar.

The day students started to pack our satchels or rattan and wicker school cases in readiness to leave. Not soon after I finished packing, I looked out the classroom doorway and saw Daeri standing in the corridor, looking over the heads of the other children in an attempt to locate me. I waved and called out to him. He immediately acknowledged and politely greeted the teacher in the classroom and said something, to which she nodded. He then came up to my desk, took over my school wicker case and told me to tell four of my classmates, whose parents were known to mine, to follow me back to our house as the police were not allowing many vehicles to pass through the roadblocks, and they might find themselves stranded at the school. Their own parents could collect them from our house.

Of course, these were exciting times for the four other classmates and me; plus the added advantage of playing together in a home environment and clearing off early from school. We piled into Dad's Austin, and Daeri drove us out of the cordoned-off roads, acknowledging the police constables stationed on duty and having to wind down the window each time to inform them of who I was and that he was taking my school friends and I home to safety. I asked Daeri what was going on. He started to explain. All five of us leaned closer towards him for better audio-visual access. Daeri informed us a bomb had exploded at the nearby MacDonald House Building, which was about eight hundred metres, as the crow flies, from our school. He said Dad had been called up for duty to the scene of the bomb blast.

MY FATHER IS POLICE, LAH!

After sending us home, Dad instructed Daeri to collect Azi from his school and Mum from her office and bring them home immediately. It was well past 6:30 p.m. when my school chums' parents arrived to collect them. In the meantime, Mum, who arrived about half an hour after we did, set about organising meals to ensure that when the other parents arrived, she could present the well-fed girls to their mummies and daddies with aplomb, just for good 'face'. Daeri was, of course, sent to locate Dad to ensure he had not become injured during the melee and was safe. Dad was fine. God was with him.

The bomb that exploded at MacDonald House, a building of red brick Neo-Georgian architecture, claimed three lives and injured at least thirty-three others. The bombing was the work of two Indonesian marine commandos who, disguised as civilians, smuggled their way into Singapore to plant the bomb during a politically tense period. Those were the days of the Indonesian *Konfrantasi* or Confrontation insurgency, with Malaysia, which at the time also included Singapore. The pair surreptitiously entered the building to plant the bomb, which was allegedly contained in a black airline canvas travelling bag. They left it on the mezzanine steps near the elevator. After igniting the fuse, the two were reportedly seen leaving on a bus.

The bomb exploded at 3:07 that afternoon, and the impact ripped off a lift door, and glass windows one hundred yards away were shattered. The saboteurs were caught, tried, and executed three days after the explosion.

When Dad related the episode to me, he said he arrived on the scene minutes after the bomb had exploded. The front pillars of MacDonald House were destroyed, and so were most cars parked around the building. The police, ambulances, firefighters and troops from the Reserve Unit, formerly known as the Riot Squad, were scampering about trying to get to injured people and endeavouring to control the ensuing chaos and prevent looters from taking advantage of the adjoining shops. In the melee, Dad caught sight of one of our neighbours, who was then a doctor working for the colonial government at the Singapore General Hospital. Dad called out to Dr B.T. Senge: "I say, BT!" Upon seeing Dad, he yelled back with a pronounced level of urgency, "Tez... Here! Over here! Come quickly!"

Dad rushed over to find the doctor kneeling beside a seriously injured young man lying on the road. The victim could hardly see what was going on because one of his eyes had been lacerated by a shard of glass from the shattered windows. Dad also bent down and kneeled on the debris-encrusted road beside the poor victim to comfort him, and Dr Senge said to the injured man, "Don't worry, I am a doctor. I have a police officer here with me, and we are going to help you." Dr Senge and Dad then carefully lifted the victim off the debris-scattered road and onto the pavement while Dad blew his policeman's whistle to summon the ambulance and medical staff to take over. The young man mercifully survived but, sadly, not the victim in the hospital bed beside him. This other victim was a Malay man who happened to be reading a newspaper while sitting on the steps outside MacDonald House when the bomb went off. That brought the fatalities to three.

Most of the teachers in my primary school were local women and trained at the local Teachers' Training Institute. In some cases, I thought of them as being well past their use-by date. The application of Oriental white pearl face powder was *de riguer* amongst the Chinese women of the day, and our ethnic Chinese teachers were no exception. We had our school uniforms, and it seemed so did they; theirs consisted of a plain shapeless *cheongsam,* also known as *qipao,* which would be tailored as a Chinese feminine body-hugging dress with distinctive features of Manchu origin, with theirs reaching to mid-calf. Then there was the signature white lace-bordered handkerchief heavily doused with *4711 Eau de Cologne* tucked into the cheongsam's frog button fastenings or tucked into the edge of the cheongsam's cap sleeves for easy retrieval. Their footwear usually was a pair of black pumps with a half-inch stubby heel, but the most conspicuous feature would be the starchy smothering of Chinese white face powder which made their already chalky pallor faces look as though they had been whitewashed. Those who required spectacles wore 'butterfly' rimmed frames. The upper part of the frames soared upwards, giving the wearer's eyebrows an sense of suspicion. The more elderly amongst the teachers had teeth that could move on command, be ejected and then retracted into their mouths. It was hugely fascinating for me to watch a set of teeth suddenly being removed and then hurriedly replaced every time a word beginning with '*Th*', '*S*', '*F*' or '*P*' was uttered. Sometimes, the ejection combined with the retraction would be unconsciously activated for no apparent reason.

 I once observed a similar dental performance by a fellow who pulled up beside our car at a traffic light. I was sitting in the front passenger seat, and Dad was driving. This chap had been focused on his car radio and was vigorously singing along to a ditty sung by some crooner. Imagining that he was a candidate vying for a place in a Talentime show, he was completely engrossed in his performance and had absolutely no idea that he had attracted the curious attention of a solitary young audience who was looking out of her car window and gazing quizzically at him. I was totally intrigued. As a measure of supplementary dramatics, at that precise moment the song concluded, he let loose his upper set of dentures, probably to give them an airing. These he ejected in one swift move and left them hanging precariously balanced on his bottom lip. But as soon as he became aware of me observing him, he quickly retracted them to minimise his humiliation and edged his car a little forward to get out of my direct line of sight.

I was fascinated by dentures; nobody in our household had false teeth. They either had good teeth, bad teeth, missing teeth, or no teeth. But I knew about dental braces because the school's Health Administration dentist suggested to my parents that I needed a set. I should, however, point out that I had an exceptionally good set of teeth. Mum concocted a recipe of toothpaste using pink tooth powder, finely crushed charcoal mixed with commercial toothpaste, and this was used as our daily toothpaste. Despite having good and healthy teeth, mine had a mind of their own, and the front four incisors had ambitions of seeing the world beyond the confines of my mouth. They started to protrude slightly, prompting the dentist to suggest braces. In those days, dental braces consisted of merely a single strand of wire strung across the entire curvature of the front teeth. The wire was attached to a pink plate of some kind of brittle plastic material, which was adhered to the roof of the mouth. This discouraged protruding teeth from growing further outwards while also aiding the closure of gaps developing between a child's growing teeth. As the children of government servants, we were availed of free dental and medical care and free public education.

Dental braces were a real impediment at school mealtimes, so during recess periods and lunch times, I would remove my braces, wrap them in a piece of exercise book paper and stuff them into my school desk. Usually, I remembered to put them back in my mouth before going home, but on one occasion I forgot. By the time Mum realised that something was missing from my mouth, it was already nightfall. So poor Daeri, Dad, Mum and I drove back to the school and summoned the watchman to open the gate.

MY FATHER IS POLICE, LAH!

Dad wore his police uniform to give the watchman a level of security comfort—after all, the watchman was also responsible for the safety and welfare of the boarding students. Dad explained hurriedly what had occurred and requested to go into my classroom to check under my desk. So the five of us, plus the school caretaker and the matron, both of whom had been summoned for the expedition, proceeded to my classroom. It was too late—the cleaning staff had already cleared all the desks of bits of paper and other rubbish, and all this would have already been sent to the school's main Garbage Disposal Unit. We were not prepared to dig into the industrial-size bins and sift through organic waste, looking for a set of child's dental braces. Thankfully, my front teeth had already straightened out by this time, and there was no further need for the use of braces, as the dentist declared.

I was very keen on the art lessons in school. From kindergarten, I enjoyed daubing with various colours and experimenting with mixing colours. Unfortunately, when I did arrive at an attractive shade of colour, I would forget what colours I had used in the mix, and if I started on something and needed the same colour shade, invariably, the object would be painted in two similar shades, but not exact matches. This accident of mixing colours was to teach me all about tones when painting a picture.

Our Art mistress was an ethnic Chinese lady, but she preferred the Western style of dress. She did, however, wear the ubiquitous 'butterfly' rimmed spectacles, which was the fashion of the day and age. During art classes, she would parade up and down the aisles of desks as the pupils embarked on their painting projects.

The initial medium was watercolours, and if she happened to pass by a pupil who was creating a promising piece of artwork, this gave her an overwhelming sense of motivation to step in and try her hand, presumably, to improve upon the artwork that the student had already begun. After she had proceeded to daub her touch on the artwork, the classmates' opinion, in all cases, was that she turned a promising watercolour into a disaster. The poor student victim would end up being totally demoralised. I always made it a point to sneeze noisily and repeatedly into my handkerchief when I noticed her heading my way. This was to serve as a form of deterrent to discourage her from continuing towards my desk, to secure her level of good hygiene. It never crossed her mind how and why the sudden outburst of sneezing mysteriously abated and ceased the moment she was a safe distance from my desk and, more importantly, my artwork. Perhaps she concocted a notion that I might have been allergic to her or her hideously overpowering cheap perfume.

The Art mistress was a peculiar individual, cheap perfume notwithstanding. I never found out whether this was anything more than an artistic temperament or if she was another eccentric like Zubaidah. When she interrupted a student's art creation, she would call for the rest of us to gather around to watch what and how she would do to improve on the art piece or demonstrate to us a supposed special artistic technique. So we would all gather around whilst she picked up the paintbrush and dabbed it first in some water and then the paint. She would then command the girls to crowd around, closer and closer to her, to get a better view, and as we did, she would then flick the paintbrush so spots of paint would splatter onto our uniforms. Then she'd reprimand, "You girls are so silly. Why did you all stand so close?"

The most devastating part of her teaching style was her habit of awarding a big fat '0' to any student who forgot to hand in her artwork the following day. This invariably had a damaging impact on some students' overall exam result averages. In those days, parents did not feel it was their right to complain about detrimental teaching techniques and teachers' unsavoury habits with schools or the Education system. It is quite the opposite case these days.

I initially found it difficult to comprehend the accent of the ethnic Chinese teachers. I had spent the two years prior to primary school attending a private kindergarten operated exclusively by a team of British women. At home, my parents spoke to us in British English, although we initially learnt to speak more Malay than English. This was a consequence of Azi and I spending more time in the company of the servants and their children than we did with our own parents.

It was reportedly recorded in my *Baby's First Book* that the first words I strung together were not 'Mummy' or 'Daddy' or anything that sounded remotely close to that. In fact, it was *Babi*, meaning pig in Malay. We also managed to glean a few choice Cantonese expressions on account of Ah Chwee's discontent with something or other. I believe it is said that the best way to learn a language is by identifying the profane words first.

Hearing words like 'the cuckoo' being pronounced as *the kakkoo*, with the emphasis on the *kakk* (rhyming with duck), or 'second' being pronounced as *seken*, or 'present' as *prezen*, 'product' was *proh-duck*, 'police' became *pooliss* came as a bit of a culture shock. Eventually, I'm sure I would have simply taken the easy way out and gone with the flow; very likely speaking *Singlish* — the unique Singaporean style of spoken English, with a patois of Hokkien, Malay and Tamil jargon thrown in for good measure, rather than the Queen's or BBC English. I think this was when Mum decided that before her children truly succumb to murdering the English language, she had better send us for elocution coaching.

Azi and I were therefore sent to an elderly Irish woman, Mrs Elizabeth Strangher, who schooled young British children for private elocution lessons. Mrs Strangher insisted that her name be pronounced as *'Straanger'*; the *'ng'* as in 'singer' and not as in 'strange', although Azi and I might argue that she was, just a little... She was a very pert and precise lady, immaculately turned out and always having her red wispy hair coiffed into a neat bun on the base of her neck. The only make-up she used was pretty pink lipstick. Even though she was probably in her mid-sixties then, she had a face and complexion that belied her years. I imagined she might have been a real drop-dead knockout in her younger years. She was a stickler for absolutely good manners and expected her students to be fastidiously punctual and meticulously neat. Mum briefed us to always be on B.B. whenever we were in her presence. Her elocution lessons, over a span of six years, assisted greatly in giving Azi and me a fair command of British English and the correct pronunciation of its corresponding vocabulary. For this, I am grateful to both Mum and Mrs *Straanger*.

After completing this elocution course, Azi and I could speak three languages fluently—English, Malay, and *Singlish,* with a spattering of Ah Chwee's Cantonese thrown in for good measure.

14

THE GRAND OLD DAME

Our favourite Saturday afternoon jaunt, without a doubt, was to be taken to a prime shopping area called Raffles Place, where our most preferred retail outlet, the Robinsons Department Store, was located. It was established in 1858 by a chap called Philip Robinson and one other whose name escapes me, and then the Store went on to become the favourite haunt of the British and European communities in Singapore. It was a three-storey, charming, awe-inspiring building with a façade not unlike that of the distinguished Harrods of Knightsbridge Department Store. Atop the building's roof stood what I believed to be a statue of a cherub almost in flight. It may have been sculpted in the image of Eros, but I cannot be sure.

In 1958 the store was awarded the franchise from the UK chain store Marks & Spencer and thereafter was deemed the 'most handsome department store in the Far East'. Robinsons was also amicably referred to as the Grand Old Dame. The original store was then operated in a similar fashion to the Grace Brothers department store featured in the celebrated British television comedy series, "Are You Being Served?" and yes, there was on every floor, the equivalent of a Floor Walker whose main function was to direct customers to the relevant departmental sections.

After the first couple of visits to Robinsons, there was no need to be told where to find what we were after. The Toys Department was on the second floor and basically occupied three-quarters of the entire floor. Mum would often go to Robinsons to enjoy Afternoon Tea with her British society friends at the Tea Room Terrace in the Store. Azi and I would be let loose, like wild animals out of a cage, in the Children's Play Area in the Toys Department. The *ayahs* would do their utmost to keep us under control but with little success. We were always forewarned to handle everything with great care because if we were to carelessly break anything, Mum was obliged to pay for it. This invariably could mean going without pocket money for months on end.

In the Toys Department, there was a cordoned-off enclosure for children to sit at brightly coloured small wooden tables and stools and play with Meccano sets, Lego building bricks, board games like Ludo and Snakes and Ladders, and partake of a host of other novelty distractions, while the *ayahs* sat on benches inside of the Enclosure's perimeter to chat with one another — compare notes, more likely of who appeared to work for the better employer and/or children. There were waitresses who periodically came around with trays of coloured plastic glasses filled with orange cordial drinks and coloured plastic saucers containing Huntley & Palmers 'gem' sweet biscuits. These were small round biscuits with a dollop of coloured royal icing on top resembling various coloured 'gems'.

As far as Azi was concerned, the most enticing distraction was a large, broad table upon which was a fully set-up Scalextric racing car track with several racing cars whizzing around and around. There was always an attendant standing by whose job was to ensure that sticky little fingers and grubby hands did not come into contact with the operating mechanisms and the

MY FATHER IS POLICE, LAH!

moving cars. As such, the boys were only permitted to stand by and watch the racing cars go round and round the racetrack, often exclaiming "ooh!" and "aah!" when one racing car overtook another. Azi was absolutely fascinated by the Scalextric set. He was given one by Mum a few months later, as compensation for a special 'event' he had to undergo, which was not a particularly pleasant experience for him, I hasten to add.

While Mum was having Afternoon Tea with her friends, Dad was usually at the photographic equipment and wristwatch departments, carefully studying the various models of cameras and watches and noting their prices.

Next door to Robinsons, there was a shop called Ben Golden & Co, which dealt exclusively with photographic equipment and wristwatches. One of the salesmen in Ben Golden & Co, Mr Wiijeyth, was also a fellow immigrant to Singapore and of 'Burgher' descent. The Dutch and Portuguese communities living in Ceylon were referred to as 'Burghers'. Mr Wiijeyth and Dad were long-time friends. Dad would then drop in to see Mr Wiijeyth and share with him the pricing intelligence he had obtained from Robinsons next door to help the management of Ben Golden & Co maintain competitive pricing levels of their products. In fact, whenever Dad had visiting friends and relatives who wanted to purchase cameras or watches, he always took them along to see Mr Wiijeyth. The only form of 'commission' Dad would accept for his recommendations was a chilled bottle of Green Spot orange soft drink beverage served to him at Ben Golden & Co.

The soft drink was offered as a courtesy rather than as a form of payment; in any case, all Ben Golden & Co visitors and customers were offered a bottle of Green Spot as soon as they entered the premises, sat down on one of the bar stools in front of the myriad of glass showcases, and asked to be shown an item, irrespective of whether they intended to buy it or not.

As a uniformed representative of the Singapore Colonial Government, particularly a senior officer of the Police Constabulary, it was forbidden to receive any gratuity from civilians, upon the penalty of immediate dismissal from the force, a jail sentence, a fine or all of the above, if convicted. Dad was a champion of integrity and diligence. He was a true stalwart of a law-abiding society and governance. However, the prospect of fiscal and other tangible temptations was rampantly availed at the relevant times.

A few beat patrol constables and other Non-Commissioned Officers allegedly did slip off the rails, so to speak, and succumbed from time to time.

Dad, however, remained steadfast to the oath he took when he joined the Police Force and diligently adhered to it until his retirement. I am proud to say that his integrity remained intact until his ultimate passing in 2014.

When Afternoon Tea adjourned, Mum would come over to the Enclosure where we were playing just to ensure that we hadn't run amok and wrecked the Store. The *ayahs* would report that nothing untoward had occurred, and with this peace of mind, she would head to the textiles department to select folds of materials for sewing curtains, frocks and other apparel and then to the haberdashery department to replenish buttons, bows and other bits and bobs for her sewing box. Afterwards, she would head to the basement floor Bargains Centre to see if she could pick up a few bargain items of clothes, linen, footwear and other household goods for the servants and their children. It was acts of kind thoughtfulness like this that nurtured and encouraged loyalty and gratitude from the servants towards my parents.

The basement floor of Robinsons also served as the Venue for the annual Robinsons Children's Christmas Party, which we attended every year. The entire basement would be furnished with rows and rows of children's tables and chairs, the tables laden with platters of jellies, curry puffs, meat pies, cream horns, chocolate cake slices, sandwiches, blancmange, and other party foods. Each place setting would have a soft drink bottle and a packet of... guess what? Magnolia fresh milk. There would also be strewn along the centre of the table Christmas crackers, party hats, and other selected children's party favours and accessories, which were safe to be used by children between the ages of five to ten years of age. Dad always ensured that the children from the Home were also treated to this Event. He made all the arrangements with Robinsons and the Home to have the children transported there in a chartered bus. The highlight of the party would be when a faux Santa Claus, appropriately dressed in his characteristic red tunic, complete with a white flowing *faux* beard, would enter carrying a sack of toys, which he distributed, one by one, to each of the anticipating children. To avoid a chaotic rampage of small hands and feet diving into the sack, each child was personally handed the gift-wrapped present rather than being allowed to dip in by themselves. This, of course, led to a certain degree of decorum and order. If any child made the slightest move to break the ranks and make a beeline for Santa, the staff in attendance would soon quell the action with, "Please be seated; Santa will bring your toy to you. Don't worry, he will not forget you." Santa was thereby spared any possibility of being mauled and his costume mutilated.

The presents were tastefully selected and not just taken from a warehouse of unsold, obsolete, or defective toys. Azi and I received toys like yo-yos, a game of Skittles, a box of toy soldiers, a doll's kitchen set, a girl's toy hairdressing set, and the like. I became quite adept at using a yo-yo. In later years, whilst waiting for my High School exam results, I took a gap job at Robinsons—

inevitably requesting to be posted to the Toys Department. I taught a few of my fellow sales buddies in the Department how to play with a yo-yo. Three or four of us would be hiding behind the shelves, trying them out. These sessions, of course, came to an abrupt halt when the departmental supervisor, one Mrs De La Guesta, who had a voice like a foghorn, would yell from one end of the room to the other, "WHAT are you all DOING back there!?"

Mum's last port of call at Robinsons would be the Cosmetics Department on the first floor. Mum was always mindful of her appearance and health and in that order. She favoured British brands of cosmetics and products and, mercifully, did not subscribe to the Chinese sort of chalky white pearl face powder popular with ethnic Chinese ladies of the times — otherwise, Dad might have got a fright every time Mum appeared with a ghoulish face emerging from the bathroom. Her trip down to the first floor for cosmetics was the moment Azi and I would be waiting for with barely contained excitement, the same sort of excitement when we were poised at various hiding places at home, ready to pounce on the thieves in a game of Police and Thieves. This was the moment when Mum would give us *carte blanche* to pick out any toy(s) we wanted within a given budget range, with instructions to our *ayahs* to escort us through the aisles of hundreds of toys to make our selection.

I invariably would choose a doll equipped with some form of unique action, or a board game to be played with the servants' children, or a stuffed animal; the latter usually being a defective one purposely selected with an eye or ear missing. When Merifa pointed out the manufacturer's defect in the toy, I would vehemently insist upon taking the defective one because no one else would take it home otherwise. Therein lies the defining essence as to why all the cats and, subsequently, dogs I homed were always strays and rescued animals.

Azi would select some sort of weaponry, which invariably would be aimed indiscriminately at some hapless target — usually me or a toy vehicle of considerable sophistication. He also maintained an impressive array of matchbox cars. Invariably the latest edition matchbox car could also be among his selected toys. We were accompanied by a young lad in a smart brown uniform embellished with two rows of brass buttons down his tunic; he wore a pill box cap with the hat strap harnessed under his chin and, donning a pair of white gloves, he would collect the packages of toys we selected, piled one on top of another until the pile was even taller than he. The *ayahs* would then volunteer to relieve the poor chap of his balancing act, and all the toys would be taken in convoy style to the main cashier, where Mum would be waiting along with her other purchases to make payment. My parents knew one of the chief accountants employed by Robinsons. Her husband was a fellow Freemason in Dad's Mother Lodge, and Mrs Lucille Buckingston would underwrite the purchases under her corporate account on behalf of Mum to avail Mum of preferential Robinsons discounts. Mum would thereupon reimburse Mrs Buckingston with a cheque, and Mum's cheques were always good.

As we exited Robinsons, Daeri would be waiting at the foot of the entrance and he and the *ayahs* would carry all the purchases into Dad's Austin which would be parked in the car park square across the way. In the meanwhile, Mum, Azi and I would walk next door to fish Dad out of Ben Golden & Co to leave for our next destination around the corner, but not before we were each offered a bottle of *Green Spot* orange drink for which we gratefully acknowledged kind Mr Wiijeyth.

Mum favoured purchasing sundry items from a grocer around the corner of Raffles Place, a shop named Sellim &

Company run by a team of Muslim Indians from Madras, now called by its original Indian name, Chennai. This grocery store was operated very similarly to the grocery store Arkwright in the British Television comedy series "Open All Hours" with the exception that Mr Sellim was not anything like Arkwright; Mr Sellim was an honest chap, did not speak with a stutter, nor pride himself as being gobby. The very first showcase at the front entrance of the grocery store was the confectionery cabinet with every manner of lollipops, sweets, and chocolates on offer. My favourites were a British brand of fruit pastilles and fruit gums. A small tube of these varieties would cost 10 cents each, which constituted half of my pocket money. A whole box of fruit gums, easily identifiable in a bright yellow box with the picture of an English boy's face sucking in his cheeks, cost fifty cents — a really extortionate amount for one with just twenty cents pocket money. I can still remember times when I would stand at the front of the showcase cabinet and looking earnestly and more to the occasion, morosely, at the luxurious fifty-cent box of fruit gums, hoping that my forlorn look would prompt the proprietor Mr Sellim to offer me the box for twenty cents. He never did — instead, he would open a large, elongated tin of cough drops featuring the face of a semi-bald-headed old geezer sneezing into a handkerchief and offer me *one* of those wrapped sweets. These were disgusting in taste — like sucking a hard blob of something which smelled like boot polish and tasted like aniseed — supposedly efficacious if one had a cough. But I did not. So not only were they disgusting, but they were also unnecessary. If she happened to be in a benevolent mood, Mum would buy me my coveted fifty-cent box of fruit gums and a huge bar of milk chocolate for Azi. This was not a regular occurrence, but when she did, it just made those Saturday afternoon jaunts all that more pleasurable.

MY FATHER IS POLICE, LAH!

Mum would be in charge of all the purchasing, whether household sundry items or personal toiletries for her or Dad. Dad used to apply a thick green, pleasant-smelling English-made pomade on his hair and favoured the use of an Indian brand of coconut oil-based shampoo. I imagined this may have been the secret behind his thick black hair, which never faded in colour for many years. Mum favoured only British-made brands of talc and toiletries, and of course, she required several bottles of the ubiquitous 4711 *Eau de Cologne*, which could well have been the only form of imported toilette water available in those days. By the time she finished her purchases at Sellim & Company, Daeri would have driven up to the shop and parked alongside, with the *ayahs* duly seated in the car. Dad would get into the front passenger seat whilst Mum and the *ayahs* sat behind, with Azi and me sitting on each of their laps. Sometimes as a special treat, Dad would let me sit in front with him, with his arms firmly grasping me around my waist. There was no legislation regarding vehicle seatbelts in Singapore in those days; first of all, there were not that many cars on the roads. Secondly, family cars were not generally driven beyond a comfortable speed of 30mph.

In 1972, the Grand Old Dame caught fire; the blaze was caused by an electrical short circuit that prompted the chief electrician to shut down the entire building's electricity supply. This of course halted the elevators, and people who were trapped inside, one of whom was a pregnant staff member, perished tragically. The fire destroyed more than S$21 million worth of goods and the entire building, leaving just the front façade standing as a grisly reminder of the epic inferno. The news headline read, "Raffles Place Ablaze!" and many smaller shops, including Ben Golden & Co, were destroyed. Robinsons was never rebuilt at its original site after the fire.

There was a long alley in between the row of shops alongside Robinsons, comtaining a horde of individual retail shops selling varied merchandise. I am not sure whether the shops in this alley were also destroyed or damaged during that fire in 1972. However, prior to the fire, this alley served as a conduit between Raffles Place and the road behind called Finlayson's Green. Well, it wasn't. It was grey in colour! This alley, called Change Alley, was jammed with all manner of small traders and retail shops selling goods ranging from cheap toys usually made in Hong Kong, plastic flowers, electrical gadgets, apparel, footwear, textiles, *sinseh* dispensaries offering a traditional Chinese practitioner's holistic medicine, cheap clothing and so forth. However, the most conspicuous, as well as annoying, of traders were the Indian money-changers known locally as *Chettiars* dotting both sides of the alley. Budget tourists sometimes patronised Change Alley but mostly it was frequented by visiting sailors. Sailors would disembark from their ships moored off Singapore and hop into one of the *sampan taxis,* small motorised wooden vessels operated by just one person that ferried them to and from Clifford Pier. The Pier served as the general thoroughfare to all manner of seafaring traffic, sailors, passengers wanting to charter a small boat to any one of Singapore's outlying islands like the sanctified Kusu Island for a picnic or pilgrimage, and even traders transporting small bales of rubber and other commodities to the nearby *Riau* islands of Indonesia.

Money changers were, therefore, in big demand in and around Change Alley. Tourists and sailors could change foreign currencies into Singapore dollars at more lucrative exchange rates than offered by commercial banks, before purchasing anything from the stalls. They could also make purchases with foreign currency from the shrewd shop operators but at exorbitant exchange rates. The *Chettiars* had no shortage of customers. They were mostly southern Indians, mercantile immigrants from the states of Kerala and Tamil Nadu.

The *Chettiar's* usual modus operandi would involve a chief 'honcho' or boss, sitting crossed-legged on a raised platform covered with a piece of linoleum with a small table in front of him. Usually bespectacled with thick round, black-rimmed spectacles and attired in a simple white short-sleeved t-shirt and a white *dhoti. He looked* somewhat similar to a cow milk coolie — except that the *Chettiars* would likely have more money and be educated. Above the table would be a light bulb dangling from a frayed electrical wire; the electricity supply was likely poached from an unsuspecting nearby shop. They were renowned for their business acumen but were apparently not the most alert of traders. I arrived at this conclusion after a couple of situations involving Azi and his near-perfect sleight-of-hand ability.

The *Chettiar* boss, whose role was to stay put at his 'station' and simply receive and dole out the currency notes for a deal, employed young 'runners', usually younger relatives, to parade up and down the Alley among the crowds with both hands outstretched, flapping wads of foreign currency notes spread out like a fan in front of them, and cry out, "Money change! Money change!" They were really pesky individuals, troublesome to both the shoppers and other stall proprietors, because they interfered with the flow of traffic. Owing to the competition, the runners had to be persistent and were always in your face, as it were. And so, it occurred that whilst traipsing through Change Alley one day, Azi decided to try out a trick. Mum and Azi were walking briskly in front, with Dad and I were lagging behind. As usual, there were runners about waving wads of money at people in the hope of catching the attention of would-be customers. The height of the projected money wads from one runner's outstretched hands came up to Azi's shoulder level and in the blink of an eye, he casually snatched a few notes from the wad, uttered a low *thank you* and continued walking along nonchalantly, as if nothing had happened. He was so quick that neither Mum nor Dad noticed what he had done. But I did, much faster than the *Chettiar* junior.

After a few more steps, the young Indian realised that he was a few notes short, and started yelling after him, "ADEY!" and rushed forward to catch up with Mum and Azi. I tugged on Dad's hand to hasten him forward to gain a clear view of what came next. This was not to be missed! Mum was completely startled when the Indian accosted them, but Azi just pulled one of his cherubim faces, looked at Mum and said blandly, "He pushed it in my face, whaaat. So I took it."

Mum was clearly not sure whether to scold him or chuckle, but she took the money out of Azi's hand and gave it back to the irate and panic-stricken runner.

"*Lain kali jangan tolak duit depan orang punya muka!*" Mum chided the bewildered runner in Malay, wagging a finger at him to warn him not to shove money directly into the faces of passersby. It sounded impressively theatrical, just as the occasion required. She then turned on her heels with her head held high and continued down the Alley with Azi, much to the delight of the surrounding shopkeepers. By the time Dad and I caught up with them, the matter had been settled. Mum related the incident to Dad and surprisingly, he laughed out loud.

A few months after the fire, Robinsons opened another store on the bustling downtown Orchard Road, but it was nowhere as distinguished and majestic as the original. It was in this store, many years later, that I was temporarily employed and imparted my yo-yo skills to my fellow sales personnel.

It may have crossed your mind why the purchase of books was not made a priority and encouraged by Mum over accumulating a senseless collection of toys. Ah. Mum was a resourceful person, you see. She made us members of the National Library of Singapore, whereupon not only did we have as many books as we could read free of charge and as often as we wanted, but we also could participate in the Library's Children's Hour Story-telling Programme whereupon children would be entertained by an hour of storytelling in a cool glass-panelled room, hosted by the chief librarian who would read aloud stories from selected books. This took place every Tuesday afternoon at four o'clock and Daeri would drive us to the Library first to select our reading books for the week and partake of the Children's Hour Story-telling Programme. I was introduced here to my first Dr Seuss book, *The Cat in the Hat,* here. So, through this channel and receiving books as birthday presents, Mum never had to purchase books for us. She envisioned that if books were purchased, once they were read, they would accumulate dust in the house. There was no need also, to send books to the scroungers—Dad's chosen word, not hers—in Ceylon, as their local schools would be providing some form of a library anyway.

With this mention of the National Library, an incident springs to mind when Daeri ferried us for our usual weekly jaunt on a Tuesday. Azi decided that he was going to be a smart alec and walk from the Library to the Freemasons Masonic Club about two hundred yards downhill from Fort Canning Road, the road behind the Library building. As Azi's Primary School was also located next door but one to the Masonic Club, he was able to persuade Daeri that there was no danger for him to walk there by himself. He knew that Dad would be going to the Club later for a Masonic General Committee Meeting, and he could accompany him home afterwards.

There was a long flight of steps from the Library car park connecting it to the Fort Canning Road behind, and once at the top of the steps, it was a short eight-minute walk to the Club. Fort Canning Road was a quiet road lined with Angsana trees, a local species that sprouted heavy branches bowing to form a thick canopy. This was also a quiet road, so quiet that the chirping of crickets and cicadas would overpower in volume any car passing by.

Azi's explanation did not completely convince Daeri, so he took it upon himself to go into the Library to telephone Dad at his office to seek permission to let Azi go. By the time he returned to the car, Azi had already left for the Masonic Club. No surprises there; after all, he was a prince and master of all he surveyed. In any case, Dad had given his consent and told Daeri to take me home first and then collect them from the Masonic Club afterwards.

When they finally returned home later that evening, Dad, Mum and Azi filed out of the car one by one, and Mum had her arm draped protectively around Azi's shoulders. There was a very solemn ambience about them all. Azi's eyes were swollen — as if he had been crying — and Dad had a very stern look on his face. Mum was silent, and Daeri looked distraught. He saluted Dad and then retired to the servants' quarters. Azi was fed, bathed, and put to bed by Mum herself, not Ah Chwee, who looked worried at seeing her charge so visibly fearful. Ah Chwee learnt what had happened from Mum, and she, in turn, informed Merifa, who then told me.

While going from the Library to the Masonic Club, Azi was followed by two older boys who had been watching our car in the Library car park. As soon as Azi started to climb the steps, the two older boys followed Azi at a short distance behind until he reached a point close to the top of the steps. One of them grabbed him from behind and pointed a pocketknife at Azi's throat, whilst the other boy relieved Azi of his wristwatch and the contents of his school shorts pockets – his pocket money and a matchbox car. Mercifully, they did not injure him and then just ran off down the other side of Fort Canning Road. As they had accosted him from behind, Azi could neither identify nor describe them.

By the time Dad and Mum arrived at the Masonic Club, they found Azi visibly shaken and crouched at the foot of the steps to the Club's main entrance, with his hands covering his sobbing face. Two of the Club's waiters were trying to pacify him, but he was too distraught to pay heed to anyone until he heard the reassuring sound of Dad's voice asking, "Azi...Daddy's here now. Why are you crying, son?" Only then did he look up and permit Dad to carry him into the car. Dad handed him over to Mum, who cuddled the terrified boy for the entire duration of the journey home. I expect Dad conveyed his apologies to the Meeting so he could return home and endeavour to coax from Azi as much information as possible about the robbery. He particularly felt guilty because he gave Daeri consent to let Azi go alone.

After Merifa told me the story that night, I waited for Azi to fall asleep. Clutching my teddy bear, I then went to his bed and crept under the covers; I slept in his bed with my arm around him and put my teddy bear over Azi's head to guard him that night. He was so physically and mentally drained that he was quite oblivious to Teddy or me being next to him. If he had suddenly woken up, he would have surely booted us both out of his bed. But as far as I was concerned, I wanted to let him know that he was still my brother despite all the bullying. I was sorry for him. And I loved him.

The following day, Dad went to Ben Golden & Co and bought Azi a new watch from Mr Wiijeyth.

15

HONOUR AMONGST THIEVES

The two thieves were eventually caught on the same road when they attempted to relieve a *Samsui* woman of her gold earrings. *Samsui* women are ethnic Chinese coolie immigrants originating from Shansui in Kwangtung Province and were easily identifiable by their trademark red headdress, a starched square piece of cloth worn as a cap. This, paired with a dark blue coarse cotton *samfoo,* which can also refer to a Chinese female's two-piece working attire, with a black apron attached in front, completed the ethnic ensemble. They wore their own style of sandals — the design more a result of poverty than tradition. The base of their sandals was cut out of disused rubber tyres, and these were fitted with rough strips of cloth or canvas across the sandal to keep it in place. They were tough women and spent most of their time outdoors. They developed coarse, weather-beaten faces and were certainly not the ladylike 'retiring little petals' as were their mistresses.

The *Samsui* women arrived in Singapore as immigrants in the 1920s and 1930s, and they usually found jobs in the construction industry. They were mostly manual labourers, cheap labourers at that. They were paid around thirty cents to forty cents a day and were frequently seen around building sites performing back-breaking errands like carrying filled baskets suspended by strong jute ropes on a single long wooden pole, balanced across one shoulder or both. These baskets were filled with bricks, earth, and other construction materials. This would be like carrying around an eighty- to a hundred-kilogram weightlifters' dumbbell for extended periods of time. They sent whatever precious little money they accumulated back to their families in China, and if there happened to be a little surplus, they would purchase a small piece of gold as an investment. Anyone even toying with the thought of accosting one of these women, let alone mugging one, was in the market for a jolly good thumping.

And so, it occurred that the very same boys had been keeping tabs on a *Samsui* woman who was sitting on the kerb along Fort Canning Road. They stealthily crept up the steps towards her and attempted to spring on her from behind. This time around, the boys had clearly underestimated their victim. This woman was totally unaffected when they pounced upon her. She brushed them off her like flies off a cream cake. Now standing upright and in defence of her precious earrings, she kicked one of the boys into the monsoon drain and planted a well-placed blow across the other boy's mouth, which caused him to lose a tooth and his mouth to bleed. Her shrieks and wails caught the attention of a few other *Samsui* women in the vicinity. The boys had no chance of escape at all. The gang of *Samsui* women fished the boy out of the monsoon drain and started slapping both of them about until they both fell into the drain again. Two *Samsui* women then climbed down into the drain and sat on the boys until the police arrived.

That is precisely how the police found them. The incident took place close to Azi's primary school and the Masonic Club, so it was not long before someone telephoned the police, who arrived within minutes. Even as the boys were handcuffed and being led into the police cars, the *Samsui* women continued to lunge at the boys and slap them across their heads whilst the police constables endeavoured to restrain these frenzied women. In the confusion, a couple of constable's peaked caps were knocked off their heads, as were some of the *Samsui* women's headdresses, revealing a stash of money, cigarettes and matches hidden underneath. These items got scattered across the road and were the contributing factor for the *Samsui* women to cease their barrage of slapping and, instead, scramble around picking up their fallen treasures.

Dad was informed of the incident and the subsequent arrests. He was summoned to the Fort Canning Police Station jail, where the duo were remanded for interrogation. After some gentle persuasion, police-style, of course, the two culprits ultimately confessed to committing a few other petty thefts along Fort Canning Road and even recalled the theft of a boy's wristwatch from an 'Indian' boy in school uniform. The stolen wristwatch, however, could not be recovered; it had been sold, and the proceeds spent on cigarettes, they confessed. Dad had initially intended to bring Azi to the station to arrange for a possible Identity Parade of the two criminals. However, Daeri, who had accompanied Dad to the station, counselled against the idea, saying it would surely cause Azi further and unnecessary distress. After all, a statement from the *Samsui* women plus the confession obtained from the thieves would suffice to bring charges against the duo in court. Daeri lingered behind at the cell whilst Dad moved on to finalising the police reports formalities. It is not known exactly what action Daeri inflicted on the pair who were confined to a cell. All I heard Daeri saying privately to Mum when they returned home was, "*Mem, itu dua orang pencuri tadi saya 'dah 'settle' betul-betul*", giving Mum a loaded hint that he had dealt with the two "investigation-style".

MY FATHER IS POLICE, LAH!

This was not the only occasion we came into contact with initial interaction with the *Samsui* women. There was a second time, this time with the distinctive *Samsui* sandal being worn on the other foot, so to speak.

One day when we returned home after a family outing, Mum noticed something not quite right about the verandah at the front entrance beneath the porch — particularly at the place where Daeri sat at the rattan table and chairs when polishing Dad's buttons and boots. Even Daeri was at a loss to determine what was the cause of Mum's puzzlement. But then Dad and I noticed the blindingly obvious empty space where Daeri's rattan table and chairs should have been. The furniture had disappeared. The servants had no idea that the furniture had vanished, claiming they were mostly indoors or at the back in their quarters. The only possible way to solve the mystery was for Dad and Daeri to go across the road to where there was a bus terminus and question the bus drivers, conductors and hawkers there, the latter doing a thriving business to a regular customer base. Mum forbade us to patronise these hawkers for fear of consuming unhygienically prepared food and thereby contracting cholera, dysentery, or typhoid and then dying. I failed to see any merit in her fear as the bus drivers and conductors seemed to be all fine from eating the hawker's delicacies. During school holidays, especially, Azi and I would cajole the servants to go across the road and purchase delectable fare like banana fritters, semolina biscuits, fried noodles, N*onya-styled* cakes, and desserts. The servants themselves, including Zubaidah too, enjoyed these very same delicacies so there was not much sweet talk or persuasion required to smuggle in this forbidden nosh.

The banana fritter hawker's stall was situated directly in front of our gate. The hawker was a young Indian fellow who fried the fritters there and then, in a huge iron cauldron of probably several times re-used trans-fat palm oil, over a wood fire stove affixed to the middle of his cart. Needless to say, all of the hawkers across the road were unlicensed and, for that matter, extremely brave to peddle their wares in front of a line of police officers' residences. Dad was not one to spoon sand into anyone's rice bowl, and as long as the hawkers did not cause any trouble, Dad was happy to let them earn a living without the threat of confiscation or demolition by the City Council. Dad, still dressed in civilian clothes so as not to alarm the hawkers when he approached them, first went to the bus company's Control cubicle to inquire whether the resident logistics officer had seen anything, whilst Daeri, who frequently purchased bananas and tapioca fritters, approached the Indian fritters hawker.

The bus officer was unable to shed much light as the parked buses in front of his cubicle obstructed his view across the road. The fritter seller, however, reported seeing two *Samsui* women enter our premises. One of them strung the table onto her wooden pole and the two chairs on each end of the other's wooden pole. The hawker shouted an "Adey!" at them, and upon hearing this, they hot-footed it out of our compound in the direction of the nearby Chinatown area. Presumably, they must have been accommodated in a small hovel in Chinatown and either needed furniture or the proceeds from its sale to supplement their living expenses.

Samsui women lived in sordid, dark, and grimy rooms, too small to have had enough space to swing a dead cat without hitting the sides. These rooms were further subdivided into cubicles above shophouses that lined Chinatown's side streets and cul-de-sacs. Each subdivided room became home to at least four women sharing one single room in which they stored their measly belongings in a wooden box, which also served as their bed at night. Their sexuality was always somewhat of an enigma, at least for anyone who was curious enough to investigate this topic. After all, four single women sharing one small room the size of a lavatory and availed of very little social companionship and entertainment... Rent in those days would have ranged from eighty cents to S$1.20 per month, and on their meagre earnings of thirty cents per day, there was not much surplus cash to indulge in frivolities or luxury goods like pretty dresses, proper shoes, cosmetics, and fancy jewellery.

Daeri asked the hawker why he had not bothered to give chase, seeing as he ought to have been supportive of a police officer who had not yet reported him to the authorities for illegal hawking. The Indian replied, "...*ada orang beli goreng pisang, lah!*" offering the lame excuse that he was serving his customers at the time. Typical. At the same time, one of our neighbours, seeing Dad and Daeri across the road interviewing the hawkers, came across to ask what the matter was. Dad, looking rather sheepish, explained with a great deal of awkwardness that two *Samsui* women had had the audacity to steal our outdoor rattan furniture, and from a police officer's residence, no less. The neighbour, who also was a fellow police officer and Freemason, asked, "Why didn't your servants set your dogs on them, Tez?"

"I haven't got a dog!" came Dad's bland answer.

"Next time, borrow mine for the occasion. Or get a couple of your own to safeguard your house!" the neighbour responded jovially, but with a mild hint of sarcasm.

This was the catalyst that led to the introduction of two mongrels into our household.

My mother's friend was into rescuing stray animals and always welcomed the arrival of potential new adoption owners. I was given the privilege of selecting just two; the first one I selected was a short-haired white dog with two black markings around his eyes, making him look more like a bandit than a panda. So, I named him Rebel. The other was a completely black female dog with long fur and soulful eyes. One of her front legs appeared to be slightly distorted at the joints, making her look like she was posing for a photograph when she stood upright. Mum named this young lady Mam'selle.

From that day forth, I always had dogs as pets.

The irony of acquiring two *watchdogs* was that they were not. Mum insisted that they had to be locked away in the garage during the night and were only let out during the day. Therefore, all potential thieves were expected to burgle us only between the hours of 8:00 a.m. and 6:00 p.m. Their diet consisted of breast of lamb cubes boiled with rice, to which Zubaidah lamented that villagers in her old kampong ate less and worse quality food.

The dogs were very well cared for and did not pose any discomfort for Daeri or the other Malay servants. They unanimously agreed that first of all, the dogs were being kept for the purposes of guarding the house—a good joke but nonetheless pertinent for its purpose. Secondly, there was no verse in the Quran itself, which forbade the keeping of dogs. As far as Daeri was concerned, there was a Police Dog Unit within the Police Force, and so our dogs in his view, were kosher to be considered and declared *halal*. I, however, pushed the boat out further; I loved these dogs and treated them as adored pets. It was therefore universally accepted that I would bathe them, feed them, and brush them every day; chores which I happily executed as there developed an enduring affinity between the dogs and me.

Merina, Sabariah and the other servants soon learnt to accept the dogs as part of the household, and we enjoyed many rounds of ball games and catch with these delightful creatures. Even Zubaidah used to bellow, "*Hoi, Rabbi!*" (Meaning Rebel) and "*Ey, Mamul!*" (Meaning Mam'selle) when she had collected all the bones and bits of gristle from our leftover food to offer them as a treat. After a while, she even showed a preference for the dogs over and above the colony of cats. The dogs knew how to be well-behaved and obedient and were always overjoyed to see any of the household humans at any given time. The cats, however, only showed displays of affection by rubbing themselves against Zubaidah's ankles when it got close to feeding time. After their bellies were full, if Zubaidah beckoned to any of the cats to come forward to her, they shot her a supercilious and contemptuous glance as if to mock, "You talking to me?"

The dogs had an arrangement with the cat colony — they would not try to steal the cat food nor accost them, and correspondingly, the cats wouldn't try to scratch out the dogs' eyes. They kept a safe and healthy distance from one another.

My insatiable curiosity about these *Samsui* women prompted Daeri to take me on an excursion to Chinatown one day, shortly after the theft of our rattan furniture; he probably using the excursion as an excuse to see if he could spot the stolen goods amongst the lodgings around the *Samsui* Women's Settlement. Upon obtaining permission from Dad, Daeri and his wife Rukiah took Merina, Sabariah, and me into Chinatown, where he parked our car along *Eu Tong Sen* Street, so named after the founder of a Chinese traditional medicine manufacturing company.

The first thing that caught our attention was a brightly decorated stage erected on stilts with many chairs lined up in rows in front of the stage. There was the sound of a high-pitched shrill singing against a backdrop of stringed instruments sawing tuneful Chinese melodies, cymbals clashing and drums beating. This would be interspersed with either a female or male voice recitative, either spoken in a sing-song style or sung as a song. We three girls urged Daeri to take us to the stage for a closer look, and as we reached eye-view, I saw men and women with garishly painted faces dressed in long colourful flowing robes. This made me immediately think of Zubaidah, who, when all dressed up, did not look as strikingly tawdry as those Chinese Opera performers on stage. Indeed, she did not—she looked worse!

We watched the performance standing at the side of the seating rows and shortly after about ten minutes of arriving, a middle-aged Chinese woman approached Daeri and told him that it would cost five cents for a ticket to watch the Chinese Opera performance, known as a *Wayang*. It was unanimously agreed that we were not going to stick around as the music and the vocal screeching were at a near-deafening pitch for the delicate ears of three young girls. Apart from anything else, we could not understand a single word. Given our lack of a capacity to understand Chinese, the story or the plot of the opera would have been for us, a complete loss. We three girls were already holding the palms of our hands over our ears to cushion the noise, so Daeri informed the lady that we would shortly be moving on. And then we left the *Wayang* vicinity.

As we walked along, I noted the various kinds of Chinese products offered for sale in the array of shophouses. A delectable aroma of barbecued meat permeated the air, coming from a shop where a bare-chested Chinese with a damp white hand towel draped around his nape was standing. He was on a wooden crate and was grilling thin slices of dark red meat on an open charcoal fire grill. I pointed to the food and asked Daeri if we could buy some. He declined the request, saying it was barbecued pork meat, and we were not allowed to get close nor touch the product. That was an extremely tall order; the aroma from the grilling meat slices was overpoweringly enticing.

There were of course the inevitable Chinese traditional *sinseh* medicine shops, and Chinese tea shops with their brews of tea varieties simmering away in large brass urns, each fitted with a tap, to fill small porcelain cups of various teas, depending on the quality required, to passing customers. And to be perfectly clear, I should mention that Chinese tea is not drunk with milk, sugar, or both. There were one or two elderly Chinese veterans with long flowing beards sitting at small wooden tables upon which was a tube carved out of bamboo and containing a bunch of flat bamboo sticks for the purposes of divination, Daeri explained. They would be flicking through an ancient-looking tome with Chinese characters written inside, presumably the interpretation of the divination sticks.

One of the old geezers beckoned to me to come forward. He smiled an open-mouthed smile revealing his mouth had a distinct vacancy for a set of dentures to be introduced. Daeri cautiously eyed the old man and, upon assessing that no harm would come of it, let go of my hand so that I could approach him. The two other girls, not wanting to be left out of the foreseeable entertainment, crowded around me to hear what the fortune-teller had to say. He asked to see the palm of my left hand and then my right. He looked up at Daeri and Rukiah and spoke in Malay with a heavy guttural Chinese accent, his voice suggesting that he was either an opium addict, possibly a tuberculosis patient, or both.

"*Ini bukan lu olang punya anak,*" he started off, "*... ini anak olang kaya punya anak*" letting Daeri know that he had figured I was not their child, and I came from a privileged family.

This last sentence made Daeri look at him suspiciously. Oh yes, Daeri must have thought to himself. Now comes the payment demand part.

The old man continued, "*...ini anak ala manyak baik punya hati. Nanti lia sulah besar hah, lia mesti manyak pandai-Oo. Semua olang suka lia wor. Manyak cantek lor, lumba one, lumba one!*", stating that I was a kind-hearted child and that in later years, I should turn out to be very smart and would be endeared to everyone. And he made a thumbs- up approval gesture.

Well, anyone can fabricate that sort of prediction just to gain favour, and Daeri thought the old man was just another charlatan. In any case, Daeri fished into his pocket to retrieve a few coins as payment and was quite taken aback when the old man declined to accept the money.

"*Ta'pa, Ta'pa,*" he said, pushing the coins back into Daeri's hands, "*ini anak bukan macam biasa punya olang,*" indicating that I was no ordinary child. Of course, we three girls thought the whole review to be a lark. I never found out what the old man meant by his last sentence. At worst, maybe my parents ought to have named me Abby, as in '*Abby-normal*'?

There were also the roadside barbers, whose furniture consisted of a rattan chair like the ones stolen from us and a small hand mirror planted on the ledge of a wall. For the princely sum of ten cents, the customer could get a haircut and shave package: five cents for just a haircut. However, the resulting hairstyle was limited to just one style—a crew cut. So, customers with ambitions of looking like the most popular Cantonese movie star of the day, or emulating an Elvis Presley hairstyle, pompadour, and all, could end up grossly disappointed after looking like a potato on a stick. What can one expect for five cents? Vidal Sassoon?

As we continued along the shophouse corridors, we heard a musical instrument being played, accompanying a shrill female singing voice. As we turned a corner, we saw an old man playing a stringed instrument, the bowl of which was balanced on his knee. Attached to the bowl was the long neck of the instrument, which had two or three strings on it, and the man used a bow to saw the strings from left to right. This produced a haunting musical sound which the female singer further accentuated. She was dressed in a colourful *samfoo*, and her face was made up with bright red lipstick and, oh yes, the white Chinese pearl face powder. I had never seen a musical instrument like this. At that age, all I knew was what a piano looked like and a dragon of a piano teacher who accompanied it. Daeri dropped a coin in another collection tin, fashioned from an old tin of milk powder which was placed at the woman's feet, and we continued on.

Further up the street, I noticed a strange-looking vehicle parked by the side of the road. It was like a small grey truck with a small cab in front, enough for a driver and one passenger, and many small doors with handles on each side of the truck's body behind the cab. Daeri explained that these trucks collected night soil or sewage from the small dwellings in and around Chinatown. None of these shophouses and hovels were equipped with modern sanitation facilities like our bungalow. Their lavatories consisted of a small room with a hole in the floor over which one squatted and emptied their bowels, the contents of which hopefully would be aimed straight into a tin bucket below. The buckets would then be collected in the morning and put into one of the small cubicles behind the small doors flanking the two sides of the truck, to be later taken to a sewerage plant for disposal or conversion into fertiliser.

Moving quickly on and away from this effluent subject, we walked further on until we reached a narrow street called Sago Street. As soon as we entered the street, I saw a large tent with a canvas canopy erected further up the street, and it appeared to be taking up half of the street's width. There were round wooden tables and chairs around them with some men playing cards. The tent was draped with long pieces of fabric panels cascading down the tent poles. These panels were in dark colours with Chinese characters embroidered on them and they were flapping about in the wind. As we drew closer to the structure, I noticed that the shophouses flanking the street had dark and foreboding interiors. I tried to peer inside one of them, but the bright sunlight outside made it virtually impossible to make out what was inside. I wondered what sort of dark secrets these places could have held, and more to the point, whether these shophouses had resident ghosts. Daeri just cautioned us to be quiet and visually take in what we saw but not to say anything.

There were fabricated paper houses, paper cars, and other household objects made out of thin strips of bamboo and paper, kept beside the tent and a large oil drum, cut in half and resting on a pair of wooden pedestals. The items on display and the goings-on around us piqued our interest to no end. It all looked rather weird and spooky to me. I looked up at Daeri with a mixture of inquisitiveness and concern and instinctively held his hand even tighter. He smiled down at me and patted my hand reassuringly. He explained softly that the tent was erected as a funeral parlour for a deceased person living in a shophouse. These particular shophouses were called Chinese Death Houses and accommodated old Chinese people who had no family to look after them in old age. This made me think even more that these places would have all sorts of spirits and ghosts hanging around. These hapless people could be labourers, *Samsui* women, opium addicts, rickshaw pullers and so forth and the Death Houses' purpose was to put a roof over their heads, both when alive and also when not.

Whilst we were standing along the street, a few police beat patrol constables filed past us and Daeri nodded an acknowledgement to them, and they likewise to him. Each time a police constable walked past, the card players at the wooden tables would cautiously look up and stare. Daeri whispered that those men were members of a Chinese Secret Society triad and rather than instigate trouble at a funeral, the police constables prudently elected not to notice the gamblers in action but just patrol the vicinity in case trouble did arise. Sitting around another wooden table were some people dressed rather peculiarly in calf-length gowns made from rough gunny sack and cotton and matching gunny sack pointed hats on their heads. They too were engrossed in a game of cards and were drinking bottles of beer.

Again I looked up at Daeri and pointed at the KKK look-alikes. These guys were the official mourners, and their job was to give the deceased party a feeling of belonging to illustrate that the departed had family mourning their loss. That is a good joke, I remember thinking at the time. How can they be sad and also be drinking beer and playing cards at the same time?

Daeri then took us past the tent, and upon looking in, I saw a long wooden structure covered with an elaborately embroidered and glittery blue shimmering coverlet. In front of the structure on a table covered with another elaborately embroidered cloth, were three large joss sticks burning, a tray with some glasses of orange-coloured liquid, a plate of Chinese buns and another with a pyramid of oranges. Right in the middle of the table on a platter was a roasted baby pig, with two red cherries stuck into each of its eye sockets. There were several small bowls of cooked rice around it. A pair of chopsticks were jabbed into each bowl, rather than being placed on the side of the bowls upon a chopstick 'rest', as is the normal etiquette of Chinese-style dining. On top of the blue-covered structure was an artificial bird effigy of some sort—not dissimilar in appearance to Boris, our ballet school peacock. As we walked past, Daeri explained that the blue-covered structure was the coffin and the bird on top of it, signifying that the deceased was a female. A deceased male would have had a lion effigy. The refreshments on the table were meant for the deceased's soul in case she should get hungry or thirsty before burial. We spent more than two hours walking around Chinatown, and this was an incredibly good learning curve for me to understand a little bit of Chinese culture.

We did not find the missing rattan furniture.

There were no more thieving incidents after the arrival of Rebel and Mam'selle, not that these canines were remotely close to being ferocious killer dogs, but in any case, I suspect it was because keeping a dog, provided it is not one of the ankle-high species, serves as a visual deterrent.

People who have encountered traumatic experiences with dogs will automatically be wary of any other dog—even a miniature poodle that would lick you to death. Rebel and Mam'selle were with us for the better part of ten and twelve years, respectively, whereupon both were permitted a dignified and natural passing when the time came.

Much to my relief, Mum did not believe in playing God; neither do I.

16

A Great Loss

My parents knew of a Muslim Malay, which they said originated in Ceylon but was not related to either of them. Nevertheless, they were both quite dear to him and referred to and addressed him as Uncle Shamat. Uncle Shamat was devastatingly poor; he was a deeply religious and pious old man and worked as the caretaker of a Muslim cemetery. He married a local Malay woman and they had one adopted daughter, Zainoona from a Chinese family. Their home was a basic structure made out of old wooden planks, with a bare cement floor and a corrugated zinc roof. There was no modern sanitation facility within the home itself and the lavatory took the form of an outhouse about twenty yards from the house. This was already a bad situation; what made it worse was their home was constructed within the enclosure of the cemetery. This meant that the lavatory was not just outside of the house, it was located in close proximity to several graves. Theirs was a house at which I made absolutely sure that I would have no urge whatsoever to relieve myself in the outhouse.

Uncle Shamat was a kind and jovial man. He never had a bad word to say about anyone and despite their level of poverty, he always welcomed visits from my parents and made it a point to request his wife and daughter to prepare and serve simple but tasty dishes. I have absolutely no doubt that my parents also supplemented their living costs with regular remittances, as it would not have been affordable for a man of his earning capacity, to have the means to provide two kinds of meat, three kinds of vegetables and flavoured rice every time we visited. Their dining table was constructed out of some planks taken out of wooden crates, supported by old unpolished wooden legs. The wooden tabletop was covered with a piece of linoleum. The chairs were also wooden and hard. Cushions were a luxury he could not afford and so Mum sewed square cushions for them, and these served as a welcome break for us when we had to sit on those wooden chairs for several hours. The three of them slept on a bare cement floor also covered with a few strips of linoleum. Despite their abject poverty, they appeared to be contented with their lot. This was home to them.

My parents were on holiday in Ceylon when the phone call came through from Zainoona. She had to walk a mile and a half to get to a public phone in order to make that call. She informed my *ayah* Merifa that her father was seriously ill, and she could not be sure whether he would survive another day, let alone a week. She did not elucidate on his ailment except that the hospital had sent him home. This is never a good omen and as ominous as it was, she feared my parents would not be able to say their goodbyes. Merifa took the decision to make a trunk call; in those days, push button telephones and International Direct Dialling had yet to make it to Ceylon. However, she was unable to contact either of my parents. In any case, they were returning in two days' time, so it was all a question of hoping that Uncle Shamat would wait for them.

Merifa, Azi and I were at the old Paya Lebar Airport late evening, awaiting their arrival. Daeri lifted me onto the railings

MY FATHER IS POLICE, LAH!

where I could see Mum standing at the luggage carousel busying herself issuing instructions to the team of porters she had summoned, as to what to do with their buffet of luggage. She had no idea what news awaited her outside. She turned and looked in our direction where she spotted me waving to her. She gave me a broad smile and returned my wave. Both of them were smiling like a couple of Cheshire cats as they exited, happy to see us. Their smiles faded in an instant, as soon as Merifa broke the news. Mum reckoned there was no time to send Azi and me home first, so we all proceeded to Uncle Shamat's place immediately after we left the airport.

Mum instructed Merifa and Daeri not to let us enter their house until she was able to ascertain whether Uncle Shamat was still with us or not. So we three sat outside on the wooden chairs, now with relief on our *derrières*, courtesy of Mum's square cushions, while Mum and Dad went into their bedroom to see Uncle Shamat. He was still alive but very poorly; he could hardly speak except for a few words acknowledging their presence. Mum then summoned Daeri and Merifa to bring us into the house and we were taken inside to see Uncle Shamat. He was lying on their bedroom floor and his entire body save for his head, was covered with a long piece of *batik sarong*. He had a thin pillow under his head. Mum brought me around to face him and this of course spooked me; I had never seen Uncle Shamat in this condition before. I knew him as the kindly old smiling man walking about, and seemingly always in a hurry to get from one place to another. Uncle Shamat always held a warm affinity towards me and used to jocularly address me as *Nonya-kuti*, meaning Little Madam. As I looked down upon this slight of a man lying on a bare floor, I must have registered a fair level of apprehension. He opened his eyes slowly and smiled at me. He attempted to lift his arm so as to stroke my face, but he did not have the strength to do so. His wife assisted by supporting his arm and then he lightly brushed my face and struggled to try and say *Nonya-kuti* before he closed his eyes again. I am sure that I saw a tear trying to escape from his closed eyelids. He was still breathing, so Mum said that we should not agitate his emotions any longer and let him get some rest. She told Azi to kiss Uncle Shamat's hand as a mark of respect and then we were ushered out of the room.

We were served plain black coffee and sweet biscuits as we waited outside for Mum and Dad to give Uncle words of encouragement and of course to his grief-stricken wife and daughter, both of whom feared the worst was to come. I expect my parents also used the opportunity to reassure them that even if that did happen, they would continue to assist them financially and even find them alternative lodgings, as a new caretaker would have to be employed to carry on from where Uncle Shamat left off. As it was getting late, my parents bid farewell to Uncle Shamat with the assurance that they would be back again in the morning to see him again. Indeed, we all did see him again the following morning, but not as an alive and active person. Uncle Shamat passed away fifteen minutes after we left the previous evening. He willed himself to stay alive so as to wait for my parents to see them for one last time before he closed his eyes for good.

By the time we arrived at their house the following day, there was already gathered a crowd of people about the house and waiting at the gates of the cemetery. The priest was inside the house with Uncle Shamat and was chanting prayers for the deceased. Both women were huddled in a corner weeping softly; it is believed that the spirit of the deceased can hear the weeping of their loved ones, and this causes the departed to feel distressed, so weeping is discouraged by Malays. Mum and Dad were the first to enter the room where Uncle Shamat was lying in repose. He was lying on what appeared to be a wooden plank and he was completely covered with the *batik sarong* which had now also been draped over his face and head. Daeri and a few other Malay males were called in to transport the body to the nearby mosque within the cemetery where Uncle Shamat would be ritually bathed and cleaned thoroughly. In the meantime, well-wishers, possibly families of the deceased whom Uncle Shamat buried during his time as the official caretaker and the Islamic minister or *imam* of the cemetery, came forward to pay their respects to the grieving widow and daughter.

Several hours before sundown, we were all summoned to the mosque to pay our last respects to Uncle Shamat before his burial. I had no idea what to expect and was reluctant to go there with my parents. Daeri held my hand on one side and Merifa on the other. Mum held Azi's hand. We walked up a short slope in between the numerous graves in the cemetery. As we walked up the slope, I suddenly had the compulsion to look to my left and that is where I thought I saw Uncle Shamat standing beside an unfilled grave, presumably his own. He smiled and waved at me. I kept looking in his direction for a few moments until Merifa, who suddenly noticed that I was distracted, asked me at what was I looking. I quickly turned around and shook my head and continued on until we came to a small building which was the *masjid*. There in the centre of the mosque's hall was Uncle Shamat completely draped in a white shroud with only his face and head exposed. His eyes were closed and there was a piece of white cloth draped around his chin and tied at the top of his head. I wondered whether he had a toothache before he passed away as it looked like a bandage for a toothache. Beside his head was a small bowl containing a sweet-smelling powder. Sandalwood powder. Mum instructed me to sprinkle some of the powder around Uncle Shamat's head, which was a sort of ritualistic requirement. I did not take my eyes off Uncle Shamat's face whilst sprinkling the sandalwood powder because I was having flashbacks of having seen him just a few minutes earlier standing along the way to the mosque. In fact, I was so engrossed at thinking about this 'vision' that I unwittingly kept dipping into the sandalwood powder and sprinkling it around his head consistently, in all haphazard directions and without pause, until the *muiz* had to gently hold back my small hands and explain that there were other's waiting behind me.

And that was the first deceased person I ever saw.

Before we left our house to go to Uncle Shamat's that morning, quite instinctively, I imagined that Zainoona would have been incredibly sad at the demise of her father. So, I remembered to bring my teddy bear with me. When we all filed in to pay our respects to Uncle Shamat at the cemetery mosque, I handed my teddy to Zainoona and told her softly, "Teddy will take care of you, and you should not worry."

I doubt very much that Zainoona was given any toys during these childhood years of her lifetime; her parents would not have been able to afford such luxuries. She looked at the teddy bear with great admiration and then dutifully handed it back with a few words of thanks. I pressed both her hands around teddy and told her that teddy was now hers to look after since she no longer had a father to look after.

I never saw that teddy bear again. He had a new owner.

My school bestie was a girl named Kartini and we were in the same class for all of our primary school years, and most of our secondary years before she was sent overseas to complete her education. We spent a lot of time in each other's houses and of course at each other's birthday parties. Kartini's father was a very well-respected renowned physician and very likely, one of the founding principals of the Boys Brigade Movement in Singapore. Her mother was probably the most artistic lady I had ever met. She had an amazing talent for floral arrangements and her culinary skills were exemplary. Both our parents knew each other very well, as Kartini's father was a fellow Freemason. Kartini and I always made it a point to sit either in front of or beside each other in class. She was academically gifted, with a remarkable talent for music and she took her lessons seriously. I was quite the opposite. Well, you know what they say about opposites attracting.

One morning, my Dad called me to him before I was about to leave for school. His face looked grave, I noted, whilst he was reading the morning newspaper. I was able to see the main headlines on the front page that revealed Kartini's father had suffered a fatal heart attack. Dad put down the newspaper and said, "Girl, Kartini's father has gone to Heaven. So I don't think she will go to school today."

I remember feeling extremely upset reading those headlines and then hearing the confirmation from Dad. "Are we going to the funeral, Dad?" I asked.

"Yes, of course, we will. Dr Arnold was a good friend of ours and I'm sure you want to see Kartini to wish her well, don't you?" he replied. I just nodded my head and then headed straight for the telephone to dial Kartini's home telephone number. There is not a lot of intelligent conversation that can be expected from an eight-year-old to a distraught grieving school chum, particularly as she was my bestie. As soon as Kartini was brought to the telephone, the only sane thing I could think of was to ask, "Are you coming to school today?"

The funeral was held four days later. Mum and Dad announced they were going to attend the funeral to be held at a prominent Methodist Church and asked if Azi and I would like to accompany them. Azi was also a school chum with Kartini's youngest brother, Reeva as they too were of the same age group. Dad said that he expected the funeral would be attended by a large number of Freemasons, local VIPs and dignitaries as Dr Arnold was a rather prominent individual in Singapore. There would also probably be an official escort of members of the Boys Brigade accompanying the cortège, possibly a parade of them lining the driveway to the Church, as well as other uniformed groups or factions in which Dr Arnold was associated and involved. "We should aim to get to the Church early," Mum started to say, "as it will probably be packed, and we might not get seating for the children."

"Right you are," came Dad's generic response, the same to most of Mum's pronouncements.

For the occasion, I was dressed in a white lace frock with white frilled socks and a pair of white leather Clarks shoes. Azi also was dressed in all white and he wore a dark-coloured boy's clip-on necktie. Dad wore a black suit with a black necktie and mum was in a plain navy-blue trouser suit. Standing in line, we all must have looked like a very morose family indeed, like something out of the Addams Family movie. Dad instructed Daeri to wear his policeman's uniform with a black armband as a mark of respect.

We arrived at the Church about an hour and a half before the scheduled Funeral Service and I noticed that as we drove up the driveway to the front entrance, there were not very many people seated inside the Sanctuary. We alighted from the car and proceeded indoors to take our seats towards the front of the altar. There was sombre organ music being played in the background and several wreaths on stands placed inside the Sanctuary. Upon looking around I was surprised that the Church did not have very many floral arrangements and, the wreaths visible at the time, were somewhat sparse, not what one would expect for a man as celebrated and distinguished as Dr Arnold. In any case, I thought that as we were so early, there would be more wreaths to follow accordingly. There was no air-conditioning in the Sanctuary and beads of sweat started to form on Dad's brow. Mum was fanning herself furiously with her black floral Spanish fan and making verbal interjections about the heat.

After about half an hour of sitting there, more people started to fill the pews and upon looking around, I noted that most of them were Chinese. I whispered to Dad and asked him whether he recognised any of his Freemason friends amongst the recent arrivals and he turned around to have a look. He said, "Not yet. They will come later. Please try and keep still, Girlie; this is a funeral we are attending, not a children's birthday party."

It was too hot to keep still. So, I decided I would riffle through the various pieces of literature tucked into the pew's pockets and see if there was anything interesting to read. Well, there was. A very significantly interesting book there, which was a Methodist Hymnal with the name of the Church printed above the words 'Methodist Hymnal'. I tugged at Dad's suit sleeve. He ignored me. So, I tugged harder. He just shushed me to pipe down. By this time, a few more people came in and some of them took the very first row of seats. This time around, I tugged at Dad's sleeve so hard that his shoulder buckled down ever so slightly. As I expected, he finally shot me one of his icy cold glares. I held up the hymnal to his eye level and said meekly, "Daaaaad, look what it says in this book. And the people sitting in the front row, I don't see Kartini and Reeva there."

Finally, this appeared to gain his serious attention. He took one look at the hymnal and exclaimed in *sotto voce*, "Oh my goodness, this is the Barker Road Methodist Church. We are supposed to be at the Wesley Methodist Church. We are at the wrong Church. Wrong funeral!" And then he stood upright like a shot and hissed a whisper to Mum, "We need to leave, NOW."

Before Mum had a chance to put up any form of contra-suggestion, Dad was already briskly walking towards the side entrance of the Church holding my hand firmly. Mum and Azi followed behind and when we were out of the Sanctuary, he explained to Mum that we were at the wrong church and needed to get to Wesley Church P.D.Q. Daeri had not parked far away and so we were on our way to Wesley Methodist Church after about ten minutes. We knew we had reached Wesley Methodist Church even before we drove up to the main entrance. There were about forty Boys Brigade uniformed troopers all of whom were wearing black armbands, lining each side of the driveway leading to the Sanctuary. The hearse had not yet arrived, and the entire Church precinct was ablaze with flowers and wreaths. We managed to get our seats in the Sanctuary and shortly after, I saw Kartini, Reeva, their mother and the rest of her family walk up the aisle and take their seats in the front pew. The pastor then ascended the pulpit and requested the congregation to stand as Dr Arnold's coffin was brought in upon the shoulders of eight Boys Brigade troopers.

After the Service, we went home. For the first time in eight years, I noted Mum's blindingly obvious silence in the car. After all, she had got it wrong.

17

A Chip Off the Block

When he turned eleven, Azi had come of age to undergo the traditional Malay, and also Muslim requirement, of having a minuscule part of his genitals, the foreskin, snipped and removed; he was due for his ceremonial Circumcision. This is known as *Bersunat* in the Malay language. This act would be the defining moment that would herald Azi's transition from boyhood to manhood. My parents had this event planned one year in advance and, depending on Azi's general health and development, decided this tradition should be carried out before he reached his twelfth birthday. Such a ceremony had to be executed with pomp and ceremonial finesse to give recognition to the young boys who were taking this step forward towards manhood.

Dad was given the task of mentally preparing his son for what was to come — I expect the fact that Dad, Daeri and every other one of the male Malays in our household had to undergo or already had undergone this procedure, to serve as little consolation. This is where the Scalextric Racing Car set comes into the picture, making a very grand entrance indeed. And there was devised, even another more glamorous incentive — my parents planned to take the family on board a twenty-thousand-tonne passenger ocean liner, the S.S. *Australia*, for a voyage to Ceylon, during the Easter holidays the following year. This sea journey would have been our second sea voyage; the first being when my parents took Azi at three years of age and I as a two-month-old baby, to Ceylon to be presented to my maternal grandmother. Mum had decided that the Event should take place at our house and not at a hospital. She was a stickler for keeping with tradition. Once the announcement was made to the servants of the forthcoming Event, every time any of them had visitors call on them, Zubaidah particularly, would glance furtively at Azi, point to him and whisper, "*Ya, ini dia*" identifying Azi as the incumbent *Bersunat* candidate.

It is a wonder that Azi did not feel like a lamb primed for slaughter. Mum had figured the best time would be during our December school holidays being the longest holiday period in the school year. Before the end of November, preparations were underway and once again, our household was abuzz with activity for the next two weeks. Invitations were sent out to virtually every single Malay in the community known to my parents, the servants, their friends, and relatives — word travels very quickly in the *kampongs,* and no one wants to miss out on a jolly good celebratory feast known locally as a *kenduri*. Today, the word *kenduri* is universally used to signify any celebratory party. These *kampong* folks were not just restricted to the villagers living in Singapore; this also included the servants' relatives from across the Causeway in the Federated States of Malaya and from Java and Sumatra. At a guess, we could expect 150 to 200 people to descend upon us. Of course, Moulana was unanimously elected to do the honours and perform the *surgery*. As he was still living at our house, this gave Azi a small but significant sense of reassurance. Azi also liked Moulana very much indeed. And the feeling was mutual.

MY FATHER IS POLICE, LAH!

Both of our schools' holidays that year commenced earlier than usual. There was muttering about our schools' curriculums being upgraded. As such, the schools had to be closed earlier so the school principals and teachers involved with the systematisation of the new syllabuses could do so unimpeded. Whilst the teachers got cracking with the schools' curriculum, Mum took time off from work to get cracking with Azi's *Bersunat* arrangements. We spent many hours traipsing around Arab Street to purchase the traditional Malay costumes for all of us. Azi had to have the finest traditional hand-woven brocade made of silk and gold spun thread, known as *songket* and this had to be spun with yellow silk and 24-carat spun gold threads: the colour yellow signifying his royal heritage. This also meant that Dad would also have to be attired in similar colours, but not necessarily in similar quality. There, she had to have custom-made ceremonial headdresses called *tanjaks*, made from silk and gold woven brocade wound into an open-styled turban. Wearing a *tanjak* is usually associated with royalty, particularly if it is fashioned out of yellow and gold threads. The final flourish had to be a solid gold and diamond-encrusted emblem in the shape of Dad's family crest, which was to be attached to the front of each *tanjak*. We went into at least five goldsmith shops walking along the length and breadth of Arab Street and with each goldsmith, Mum could not seem to get the required emblems created at the right price.

After several hours of shopping, we became hungry, and Dad suggested we go into one of the Islamic restaurants to have a late lunch. The nearest restaurant we happened upon did not meet with Mum's approval, so we went to look for another one. The second one we passed did not have too many people in it so Daeri surmised that the food couldn't be all that good. Believing this to be a valid observation, Dad then suggested we look for something else. We then happened upon a restaurant which served Indonesian food—right up Daeri's street. The adults unanimously agreed that this was a good choice and happily we entered and sat at a table. The restaurant was not particularly of a top-notch standard and the advantage was that we did not need to wait for the food to be cooked first. The various types of curries and a buffet of delectable spicy dishes originating from Padang in Indonesia, collectively known as *Nasi Padang*, were already prepared, and set out on display in a glass showcase placed on top of a wooden cabinet—we only had to go to the showcase and point to what we wanted.

As Dad and Daeri were lumbered with carrying all the shopping bags, Mum graciously invited them to go ahead first to select their food. As they approached the cabinet, I watched in mute humour as a rat the size of a small cat suddenly emerged from underneath the cabinet display of food and scurried across the floor. As I tugged on Mum's arm to draw her attention to it, another one darted out from beneath the cabinet, and this of course confirmed exactly what I had seen earlier. This time around, Mum also caught sight of the rodent in full flight. In one fell sweep she abruptly got up from the table, snatched us two children, one in each hand and marched briskly out of the restaurant, much to Daeri's and Dad's bewilderment. They were both holding an empty plate each just about to scoop in some food. "There are RATS in this establishment!" Mum shrieked. "We are leaving NOW!!"

Dad's and Daeri's disappointment was more than evident. Mum just kept on marching out briskly without stopping or looking back. As far as she was concerned, we should all starve rather than eat rat-infested food. Dad and Daeri soon followed carrying the shopping bags, and we all piled into the car and started on our way home.

MY FATHER IS POLICE, LAH!

"You'd better get the police to close down that restaurant" Mum said. "Think of all the people who could get typhoid and cholera from a place like that!"

"That is not a police concern," Dad replied calmly. "That's a health and environment issue. I don't have the jurisdiction to tell the proprietor so."

"Well, you'd better get the authorities to do something about it," she retorted. And so we returned home tired and hungry. The sum total of our day had been centred around *songkets*, *tanjaks*, and... rats.

Several weeks prior to the ceremonial date, Dad had commissioned a Malay traditional group of musicians known locally as a *kompang* group to play the *rebanas*. These are hand-held flat drums which are rhythmically struck by hand and not a pair of drumsticks. This beating of drums was to herald the arrival of the *Hero* to the Ceremony. A large canvas tent structure had to be erected to accommodate the tables and chairs for the well-wishers and visitors, as well as the construction of a raised stage, enveloped with fancy embroidered curtain material draped down the front, sides and back and coloured lights strung around the entire front façade of the stage. Inside, the stage was a small, light, and raised platform with steps leading up to it, which was fully carpeted. Another small lightweight raised dais over this platform was added on top and also covered with short pile carpeting, bright yellow satin material. A large matching satin cushion was to be placed upon the dais where Azi, treated as a *King for the Day* would be seated, dressed in Malay traditional finery. Here, he would receive the greetings and compliments of the visitors before the actual Event took place.

There was also the catering to be considered, for at least a two hundred-strong crowd of visitors, excluding members of the immediate family and the servants. Zubaidah volunteered to oversee the catering when the time came, as long as Dad provided the massive cauldrons and utensils for preparing food for feeding such a multitude of mouths. As such, Kebun fenced off an area in our generous courtyard, where these large cauldrons were going to be placed. They were each placed upon six equally large charcoal- and firewood-fuelled stoves. Dad had ordered several hundredweight of gunny sacks containing firewood and charcoal. These sacks of kindling and coal were piled one on top of the other along the length of the courtyard. Dad was mindful not to have the chickens or the other farm animals slaughtered on our premises for fear of traumatising me. So the ready-plucked chickens and huge chunks of meat were purchased from the Kandang Kerbau wet market and sent to our house *en masse*.

Kandang Kerbau, which simply means Cattle Enclosure, was the name given to the area where presumably, a modest number of cattle was initially reared in days gone by. The name was also given to a large maternity hospital in the area, and the Kandang Kerbau Hospital was the place from where we first made our entrance into the world. Notwithstanding being associated with a herd of cattle by virtue of our place of birth, our claim to fame is that we were delivered by a gynaecologist, Professor Benjamin Sheares, who in later years was elected to be the Republic of Singapore's second President.

Scores of large round enamel platters, almost matching in size the diameter of the table tops, were brought in. These platters, loaded with yellow spicy flavoured rice known as *buryani* or *pilau rice*, curried chicken and meats, cucumber pickles and various types of vegetables would be placed in the middle of each round table for the guests to partake in a communal style of dining on the day itself. This conveniently dispensed with the need for singular plates and cutlery and correspondingly, the

MY FATHER IS POLICE, LAH!

mishap of encountering breakages or missing cutlery.

The drinks to be served had to be absolutely non-alcoholic, although Dad kept a stash of whiskey camouflaged as tea stored in a few teapots, reserved for his drinking chums to partake in after the Ceremonial activities had concluded and the Muslim guests were gone. The non-alcoholic beverages consisted of a mixture of rose syrup diluted in water, in which *biji selasih* (basil) seeds were soaked until they expanded and resembled frog spawn. These seeds were said to have a cooling effect in quenching thirsts in tropical zone temperatures if one was able to disregard the frogs' egg's connotation first.

There is a Malay expression, *gotong-royong*, which refers to an act of joining forces to get a task done and which entails everyone usually volunteering, or sometimes getting forcibly roped in, to contribute towards an activity or in this case, festivity. And so began the mammoth task, two days before the big day, the peeling gunny sacks full of onions with the corresponding teary eyes that followed, the pounding of dry ingredients, washing of barrels of uncooked rice, plus the chopping of chunks of meat from probably sixty chickens, two bulls and six goats, and of course the back-breaking enormity of cleaning up afterwards. There was a flurry of human traffic to and from the master kitchen and of course, no *kenduri* preparation in our house would be complete without hearing Zubaidah's shrieking voice in full force.

Absolutely every single one of our servant population was called in for duty and they, in turn, also called upon relatives and recruited some *kampong* folk from their respective *kampongs*. Mum every now and then would simply step into the courtyard to inspect the proceedings and ensure that all was going according to plan—her plan, and not Zubaidah's. Daeri's main task was to ensure that Azi did not suddenly chicken out and bolt. Presumably, the prospect of the Scalextric racing car set was enough incentive to make him stick around and go through with it. Moulana also did his part by consoling the boy; he reassured Azi that he would use his Sufi magic skills whereupon the actual circumcision would cause Azi to feel no more than a small ant-bite and he would be romping around, as usual, the following day--and be the proud owner of a new Scalextric Set as additional incentive.

The day before the Ceremony, Azi was encouraged not to drink too much liquid so as not to give him an overwhelming urge to urinate after the circumcision took place. Moulana went to the back of our house to select a banana tree. After uttering some prayers to the chosen tree, he instructed Kebun to cut down the tree and separate the trunk from the broad leaves and unripe fruit which could be used for cooking. The trunk was to be cleaned and polished to remove any bits of dirt, debris, and loose fibres. This would later be taken up to the prepared stage and placed near the dais, where Azi would be sitting on the cushion. A complete betel nut feast of areca nuts, betel leaves, slate lime, and other betel chewing condiments was placed on an elaborately carved solid silver tray and had to be brought up to the dais. Zubaidah insisted on doing this, despite Kebun telling her that the dais would not be able to support the bulk of her weight; it had been designed and constructed only to support an eleven-year-old boy's weight.

You can never force someone to accept a good piece of advice that they are not prepared to receive; the eyes become useless when the mind is blind. Zubaidah was heavy and as she carried the betel tray, the dais gave way and she sank into it with both feet, like quicksand, and then her large posterior landed heavily on the remnants of the dais with a heavy plonk. "*Oh Mak Puchok Meletup!*" she exclaimed in dialect gibberish, as she went downwards, and the tray flew upwards. The calamity saw all the condiments, betel nut assortment, containers, and the tray land within a three-foot radius around the now cluttered stage. Kebun had to apologise profusely to the contracted workers and appeal to their generosity to rebuild the dais. The workers found the whole scenario hilarious and agreed to repair the damage at no additional cost to Kebun or Dad. They may have considered the comedy of errors priceless and well worth the inconvenience of a bit of extra work. Poor Kebun then had to try to unwedge his wife from the collapsed dais and pick up as best as he could the fallen debris from the betel nut tray. The crestfallen Zubaidah, cursing and muttering under her breath, limped off the stage, rubbing her generous backside as she waddled back towards the master kitchen.

The workers started on the repair work whilst cracking all kinds of ethnic-flavoured jokes, too complicated to be translated, and relating to Kebun's crackpot of a wife, and muffling their laughter. When Mum came to know of the calamity, she pursed her lips and sighed, "I have a headache this big with that infernal woman's name on it," she said, demonstrating with her hands two feet apart from each other, "If she cannot be part of the solution, she will either be part of the problem or create a problem with every solution!" Mum's wit and wisdom was boundless! There were no further mishaps after this. Zubaidah was too embarrassed to show herself again.

On the morning of the Ceremony, the visitors started arriving at around 7:00 a.m. The Ceremony was to begin at 10 a.m. All around the house was draped with colourful buntings dancing in the breeze and coloured light bulbs giving the house a most festive ambience. The grounds were dotted with colourful sprays of *bunga manggar*, the Malay traditional festive decorations. Large pineapples with their prickly crowns hacked off served as the radial base into which the skewers of *bunga manggar* were pierced. The simulated flower in bloom on the pineapple was then mounted upon a brightly painted pointed pole which was stuck into the ground or lashed to a pillar or tree trunk. The *kompang* players were in position and just awaiting Azi to descend before they would beat their drums in a syncopated rhythm, and sing songs in Arabic, to announce his arrival.

Azi was given a special bath by Moulana himself. The bath water was infused with various herbs and lotions prepared by Moulana and this presumably was to act as a sort of pre-antiseptic and anaesthetic wash. Azi was then dressed in his new attire and bedecked with gold ornaments and jewellery. A lavishly decorated sedan chair was brought in to parade him outside to all the visitors and well-wishers. Mum, Dad, and I also had new traditional-styled clothes for the Ceremony. Being a part of Azi's family, we escorted him along the route wherever he was carried, whilst Mum and Dad smiled proudly, nodded their heads and accepted the outstretched hands of the guests as an acknowledgement of reciprocating their *Salaams* and greetings to the assembled guests. All the servants, including Zubaidah who appeared to have fully recovered from the previous day's blunder, wore the new clothes Mum had purchased for them and everyone looked very stylish and smart indeed, especially Azi who looked regal.

As soon as Azi was ready to emerge, the *kompang* players started to beat their ethnic drums or *rebanas* to commence the processional anthem and Azi emerged before the crowd seated on his sedan chair, carried by Jaafar, Harris, Daeri, and Zainal, all dressed splendidly in their traditional Malay outfits. Moulana, dressed in his priestly robes and regalia, preceded the procession swinging a specially suspended charcoal brazier burning with frankincense as he led the way. The rest of us followed behind taking in all the greetings, well wishes and smiles from the visitors, particularly receiving the green envelopes of money designated for the Hero. It would not have been difficult for anyone to easily mistake the Occasion as a coronation, rather than a *Bersunat* Ceremony.

As soon as Azi finished his rounds he alighted from his sedan chair and was duly escorted by Dad and Daeri, the latter holding a yellow ceremonial umbrella over Azi's head. They walked up to the stage where Azi took his place and sat cross-legged on the square cushion on top of his special dais — a new one replacing the shattered one of the previous day. The rest of the retinue then followed him up the stage and we sat on the carpeted floor, flanking the King for the Day. Moulana then ascended to the stage and sat across from him. He then commenced the proceedings by invoking God's Name and recited some prayers and religious chants. The *kompang* drummers then ceased their drumming as one by one, the visitors filed up to the stage to acknowledge Azi and offer their *Salaams* then filed down again in an orderly fashion. I then observed Moulana taking the salver of condiments and handing Azi a small dish of what looked like chocolates, inviting him to eat a few. As I watched Azi, I tugged at Mum's sleeve and asked, "Can I also have some?"

"Sshhh…" she hissed, holding her finger to her mouth, "… these are special chocolates not for little girls, okay?" She softly brushed the hair away from my forehead and secured it with a bobby pin extracted from her own coiffure.

Moulana continued to recite holy verses and chants and then he stood up holding the frankincense brazier and circled the incense around Azi's head three times. He then gestured to the retinue that it was time to leave the stage. As we filed down the steps, I saw Daeri and Kebun placing the banana tree trunk on the middle of the stage and hand to Moulana another large tray bearing some yards of white cloth, a small salver of what appeared to be ointments in small containers and, a long velvet bound case. As soon as we had descended, Moulana pulled the curtains across the stage leaving just Azi and him alone in the enclosure. Mum took me into the house and told me not to disturb Azi for the rest of the day. Before she could finish the sentence, I heard Moulana's voice exclaim in Arabic, "God is Great!" and then silence. No sound from Azi. No more sound from Moulana.

I looked nervously at Mum and the other women servants. They were smiling at each other and did not appear to look too concerned. On the strength of this, I presumed I still had a brother. I quickly ran upstairs to my bedroom to fetch my new teddy bear, as a source of comfort. My previous teddy bear of course, now had a new owner, Zainoona. Mum and Dad then proceeded to entertain the guests; Dad particularly was engaged in fussing over the arrival of some of his British counterparts from the Police Force, fellow Freemasons, and their wives, who had turned up for the Ceremony. They were ushered to the main dining room inside the bungalow, separately from the dining seating arrangements of the Muslim Malays seated outdoors. At the dividing point of the Dining Room and the Living Room, a large Chinese Blackwood and mother-of-pearl inlaid lacquer screen was placed so as to conceal most of the Dining Room area from the Living Room. The large dining table had special place settings laid out for the non-Malays, and the mysterious teapots accompanied by small glasses and a large ice bucket suddenly made an appearance.

The Ceremonial Stage remained curtained until Moulana descended the steps and instructed Azi's attendants, Daeri, Zainal, Jaafar and Harris, to bring food and drink and keep him company. Moulana then fetched Mum, Dad, and me to visit our

MY FATHER IS POLICE, LAH!

Hero. When we ascended the steps, I saw Azi with his head on the satin cushion, lying on his back on the carpeted floor. Around the lower half of his body, he had a sarong with the front part knotted and tied with a cord and suspended upwards. This elevation of the *sarong* was like a small tent above his lower body, strung by the cord over one of the stage's beams. Mum was the first to rush to his side. "Are you all right, son?" she whimpered with tears almost welling in her eyes. He turned his head slowly and looked past her at me. He gave me a weak smile. I had a teddy in my hand, and I brought it to his side. "Don't worry," I said comfortingly, "Teddy will guard you." Moulana was standing nearby. He knelt down beside Azi and said, "Son, regard her well—your little sister will look after you all your life." Little did either of us realise that these sagely mysterious words uttered by Moulana would one day come to pass, many years down the road. He then arose and went over to Dad, who was waiting to approach Azi. He said softly, "Brother," he addressed Dad, "this girl is no ordinary child. She has been sent to you by, and for, a very special reason. I am sure you already know this exactly."

His comment made me think about my encounter with the Chinese fortune teller in Chinatown, to wit, this remark from Moulana could well have been another indication of the '*Abby*' as in the '*abby-normal*' stigma. I watched the expression on Dad's face after Moulana had spoken to him. He and Mum appeared to exchange knowing glances at each other. They appeared to know precisely what Moulana meant. If any of those three had taken the trouble to explain it to me as well, then all four of us could have been privy to this knowledge.

The revelling progressed throughout the rest of the day and soon after lunch, the Malay visitors started to disperse. A few hangers-on, mostly women, lingered behind to partake of a communal betel-chewing social, with Zubaidah playing hostess.

Kebun had spread a large reed mat on the grass and these ladies sat cross-legged and several betel chewing trays were brought forth with the indispensable spittoons. Gossip prevailed as did much laughter, exclamations, and a few choice curses just to add a bit of spice to the camaraderie. The Malays are truly a sociable, convivial race of people and will make the best of any opportunity to make merry. Once the chatter and betel chewing were well underway, the *kompang* group joined the ladies. A dance session featuring a type of Malay social dance originating from a Portuguese country dance called a *Joget* commenced. Malay women and men danced together to the rhythm of the beating *rebanas* and the *kompang* players had the skill to make their *rebanas* not just play a rhythmic beat in harmony, but to generate a musical sound of an Arabic tune being played. They would sing traditional ethnic songs to the accompaniment of the rhythmic beats. Zubaidah was in her element, not realising how comical she looked waddling her generous posterior about from side to side whilst flapping her folded arms to resemble wings. From where I was watching, her dance movement was aimed at emulating the *Joget*. It did not. Hers was the *Funky Chicken*. And she was about to lay an egg.

Wasn't it Coco Chanel who was quoted as saying, "You live but once; you might as well be amusing"? As long as Zubaidah was happy, so was Kebun.

As sunset approached, most of the Muslim Malays had already left and it was time for Azi to be taken down from the stage and to bed. His lower body was still draped in the sarong, which was held extended outwards in front of him, so as not to abrade with his recently inflicted wound. Moulana led the way with Mum, Ah Chwee and Daeri following closely behind, carrying his earlier donned regal robes and paraphernalia. As he was brought into the house, I made a most heart-warming

MY FATHER IS POLICE, LAH!

observation which drew my immediate attention—Azi was holding my teddy bear. I guess when a person hits an emotional rock bottom, even the smallest act of kindness from a sibling, or any other person for that matter, does hit home and registers with the softer side of the person's emotional psyche.

Dad in the meantime, was in his element, playing the perfect host to his British guests and oozing with his signature gentleman's charm. By this time, he had decided that it was safe enough to dispense with the mysterious teapots and some familiar labels on bottles emerged from his liquor cabinet. There was much chatter and laughter amongst them, I expect as a result of the copious amounts of alcohol being consumed since afternoon tea time. As far as I can remember, during any of my parent's social functions held at our house, all of Dad's British friends and associates held their drinks very well, as did Dad.

I do not recall a single incident of over-inebriated behaviour from any of them. There might have been the occasional wife fluttering her eyelashes at someone else's husband, but this sort of casual behaviour occurred generally on account of the British women in Singapore being depressed with their lifestyles, to wit, having to contend with living in the heat-addled tropics, being away from Blighty, and unable to cope with several varieties of Asian cultures and customs in one place.

Many of the colonial wives became expert Bridge or Whist players, and alcoholics as well, on account of the regular card games' sessions accompanied by the notorious gin & tonics that followed. But the men had full-time jobs and, in most cases, were stationed in senior postings and as such, the gentlemen were just that. All of Dad's colonial gentlemen friends and peers were also Freemasons. There was a Code.

The following morning, Azi was awakened bright and early so as to have himself cleaned by Moulana. As was expected of

Moulana, whatever magical balms and ointments he had applied to Azi's wound the day before appeared to have done the trick. Azi was miraculously walking about as if it was just another normal day for him, but Moulana did caution him not to take it too far, as the medication applied to his wound only served to eliminate any discomfort, pain, and to aid quick heal quickly but not completely in twenty-four hours. He would have to wait another twelve days before he could expect to ride his bicycle, at least.

But this was not Azi's main focus; there was a Scalextric set awaiting installation, and this could not wait. As he walked past me, he shot me one of his renowned menacing glares, as if to warn me to stay away from him and his Scalextric set. He was back to normal.

18

CROSSING THE EQUATOR

Our next long school holiday, the Easter break, occurred shortly before my ninth birthday. As was part of the *Bersunat* Ceremony package, Azi was also promised an ocean voyage to Ceylon on board the S.S. *Australia*, a 20,000-tonne passenger liner that would be passing through Singapore from Australia to pick up passengers. The vessel would then proceed directly to the port of Colombo before heading west across the Equator to its final destination, England, after making a few more ports of call on the way.

Preparation for the voyage itself was an adventure. First and foremost, Azi and I cautiously ensured all toys were in our toy room and none were lying about out of barracks to avoid Mum espying and confiscating them. All confiscated toys would then be heading to Ceylon to our ever-anticipating relatives. We had precious little control over our clothing, so it was a case of what will be, will be. Whatever items of clothing we should lose to the relatives would have to be replenished accordingly and in equal numbers, style, and quality lest Mum should be on the receiving end of any adverse comments from her friends and peers about the state of dress of her children.

As we were travelling by ship, there was no limitation on the number of luggage pieces or their total gross weight. So Dad was commissioned to go out and purchase five ocean voyage steel trunks. None of the servants would be accompanying us, apart from our *ayahs,* Ah Chwee and Merifa, who themselves were extremely worried about the sea voyage. Neither could swim, and both envisaged us paddling all the way to Ceylon in a roughly constructed wooden canoe, like a *sampan*. Obviously, Mum would be orchestrating the packing for the entire family whilst the two *ayahs* were left to do their own. This, of course, was a very welcome prospect for an inquisitive-minded child, to be able to see what interesting titbits the *ayahs* had in their possession.

The first room I visited was Ah Chwee's. On account of her ethnicity and belief in the Goddess of Mercy Kwan Yin, she was the more intriguing of the two. I watched how she carefully laid out several of her *samfoo* and trouser sets neatly on her bed. She then took out some items of hair accessories, a white fine-toothed comb, and a small metal box in which she had an array of buttons, needles and threads of varying colours and sizes. She then removed some squares of black coarse cotton cloths. They had a most daunting offensive smell and I asked her what those pieces of cloth were. She did not answer me, but she simply folded them and placed them into a square of brown paper which she then tied up with a bit of string. I did not try to pick up nor poke the package for further investigation. For one, I did not want to agitate her for fear of being chased out of her room and secondly, they stank. That brown paper could have been wrapped around something dead. But I kept staring at the package until Ah Chwee finally relented and said, "Girllee-aah, one day you become a *big girl*, then you also need to use." At the time, I had no idea what she was talking about. I asked Mum what Ah Chwee meant by *big girl*. She simply replied I wasn't there yet and still had a long way to go.

Rukiah finally explained that those black pieces of coarse cotton were used by grown-up women once a month during woman's *sickness*, which occurs when little girls become grown-ups. The black cloths were the equivalent of modern-day sanitary napkins. Before the advent of modern-day sanitary napkins and tampons, local women in the 1950s and 1960s used pieces of folded black coarse cotton cloth, routinely washed and dried for re-use. I expect the Samsui women would have used the same form of sanitary napkins, if not having to resort to something worse, like cut-out pieces of rubber tyres. Fortunately, the archaic black cloths evolved into commercially made sanitary napkins and tampons.

Ah Chwee then carefully wrapped the smallest of her three *Kwan Yin* statues in a clean piece of red cloth and she secured the wrapping with a long piece of gold thread. She did not place the statue in her suitcase; she placed it in her handbag, which consisted of a wicker woven basket with an overlapping flap secured with a metal clasp. When I asked her why she did not put the statue with the rest of her clothing, she explained that in order to be respectful to the Goddess, it was not prudent to place any Deity's statue together with items of underwear and footwear, as these items are worn over the lowlier parts of the body. Also, it was not permissible to allow the statue to be placed on the ground, as would be the case if it were to have been packed in her luggage. She would always be carrying her handbag so she would be in control of that. She could ensure that her handbag was never put down on the ground.

Merifa's room was something quite extraordinary. It looked like a cross between Aladdin's Cave and Change Alley. There were so many things in the room that I wondered how she knew where to find anything. I expect that there must have been a method to her madness. Her room cabinets were overflowing with all manner of artefacts, so many that she had to struggle to shut the doors tightly on the bulging cupboards. I had absolutely no idea about the number of shoes, slippers, and sandals she had accumulated; she could well have been in competition with Imelda Marcos. She had a maze of costume jewellery and beads; she was evidently conscious of her complexion as she had several bottles of creams and lotions in every nook and cranny in her room. She did not require a bed as she slept in my bedroom. She therefore took this opportunity to fill every conceivable bit of space in her room with all her possessions and chattels in the expectation that one day, she would be taking all this back with her to Ceylon when it was time to be married. I did not want to hang around to watch her packing, lest some hidden rodent or despicable creature should suddenly spring from one of her cabinets. I left in a bit of a hurry.

We arrived at the Keppel Docks in good time, and it was daunting to see such a large vessel as the S.S. *Australia* berthed alongside the wharf. Looking up at it, I simply could not see the top of the ship. It was as if it disappeared into the sky. I had never seen any real-life ship before, only in photographs and picture books. Our luggage accompanied us in a lorry that Dad had to hire to accommodate and transport the five steel trunks. Mum stepped out of our car in all her elegance and poise, like a film star about to embark on one of the Cunard ocean liners; and she certainly did look the part—after all, if you are not one, then at least try and look the part. The two *ayahs* busied themselves sorting out their own luggage and, taking in the magnificence of the ship for themselves. Dad was in charge of all the registration and documentation, so the two *ayahs*, Mum and I went into the passengers' waiting room for Dad to complete the formalities. Both Azi and I could not contain our excitement. As we feared the retribution of a voyage cancellation threat for any form of bad behaviour, we stayed put and sat quietly.

Mum, Merifa and Ah Chwee were terrified of walking up the gangway onto the ship. The gangway was placed at a steep angle and was rather high in elevation. In those days, gangways were not designed quite like the hi-tech modern ones used for passengers boarding the Cunard Queens at the Southampton docks today. The old gangways were rather bouncy, made of wooden planks sealed together and supported by metal rods, with wires threaded through to serve as support railings. A long piece of canvas bearing the ship's name would be fastened to the sides of the railings. Owing to their inability to swim, they did not relish the prospect of slipping off the gangway and falling into the sea. The three of them unanimously decided that it would be safer all around if they were to enter the ship through the lower tradesmen's access. This was where all the food and beverages and luggage and other amenities were brought on board by the wharf-side coolies. Dad had to use his best persuasive tactics to convince Mum not to use the tradesmen's entrance lest she *let the side down*. Apart from anything else, she would be letting her poise and dignity take a steep dive, mingling amongst the coolies. He said it would be all right for the *ayahs* to use that access, but not her. I guess the words *'poise'* and *'dignity'* must have struck home and she ultimately agreed to use the proper passenger gangway, as long as a uniformed ship official led the way and Dad would be directly behind her to stabilise her ascent. Azi and I embarked on the vessel by the passenger's gangway, behind Dad, looking over the sides of the gangway railings to try and gauge the altitude of the steep drop. Children know no fear.

My first impression of the ship's interior was the smell of fresh paint; the same smell as in my kindergarten and the Red Shoes School of Ballet. So this made me feel a little nostalgic. This ship was by no means anything as luxurious as the Cunard ships of today, indeed not even of those of the same era. But as far as embarking upon an ocean voyage was concerned, this ship was completely adequate for two wide-eyed and excited children who had never been on something of which we only knew in picture books. I was not aware of whether there were different classes of cabins. In any case, I could not care less; I was going on an ocean voyage!

We walked through long corridors and up a series of steps before we arrived at our cabins. Dad had booked three cabins: one for him and Mum, and the other two for us twin-sharing with our *ayahs*. My cabin had a larger porthole, and I was allowed to take the upper bunk with Merifa on the lower one. There was a small bathroom tucked away in the corner and a slim wardrobe beside it. Merifa unpacked some of our clothes and tucked away the empty luggage underneath her bunk. Azi's cabin had a smaller porthole for some reason. He barged into my cabin through the connecting door to inspect my cabin's porthole and upon seeing that I had a bigger one, he decided that this would not do at all. He insisted that we switch cabins and I refused. He was so adamant that we switch cabins that he tried to wrestle me out of my top bunk with such force that I almost fell to the floor. Suddenly there was a loud *smack* sound from behind Azi. Dad had heard the raucous bickering and appeared out of the blue. He gave Azi a sharp blow on his buttocks, which took the boy, Merifa and me, quite by surprise. That was the first time I had ever seen my Dad raise his hand to his son and heir.

The voyage to the port of Colombo was going to take twelve days. This was going to be twelve days of no school, no homework and above all, no piano lessons. The next twelve days were going to be sheer celestial bliss. It took about two days for Ah Chwee to find her *sea legs* and get accustomed to the movement of the ship.

MY FATHER IS POLICE, LAH!

Merifa, Dad, and even Mum had no problems with the ship's listing and we often took long strolls along the deck to take in the sea air which, Ah Chwee told Mum, was exceptionally favourable for her mild sinusitis. During the afternoons, whilst my parents took a nap, the *ayahs* were instructed to take us to the Children's Playroom. A mousy-looking European lady was in charge of the Playroom. She was always wearing the same sweater draped around her shoulders every time we went there, the same sweater every day for twelve days. Gosh, it must have stunk. It did not occur to me that the sweater could have been part of her uniform and that she could have had several of the same. She looked up and nodded every time we came in and then continued reading her book. The room had lots of board games, modelling clay, children's books, a fully furnished doll's house, Meccano sets, a wooden box full of Lego bricks and a train set, but no Scalextric racing cars, which Azi missed terribly. Azi and I dabbled with the Snakes and Ladders, Ludo, and Chinese Chequers board games, and then we each went our separate ways, he to take a stab at the Meccano, trains set and Lego, and I went to the doll's house and read the children's books. Everyone was happy. Mealtimes for us were restricted to the cabins, whereupon Mum would order food for the *ayahs,* and from the Children's Menu to be brought to us in our cabins. My parents went to dinners dressed to the nines, and after dinner, I expect they partook in the ship's social activities of which we knew little, as we were in bed by 8:00 p.m. sharp. The journey was pretty much smooth and peaceful, except for one dramatic event.

As the ship was crossing the Equator, the ship's crew organised some kind of a festivity to commemorate the Crossing and selected passengers who were crossing the Equator, were invited to sign up to join in the fun. I was not aware of this. There was a huge gathering centred around the ship's swimming pool and at one end of the pool deck were some crew members dressed up in peculiar costumes and they had garish make-up painted on their faces. One in particular looked like an oversized blob of seaweed with arms flailing about, and a crown upon his head—a cross between an octopus and a large blob of seaweed wearing a crown upon his head. Dad explained that the *royal seaweed octopus* was supposed to represent King Neptune. As we appeared to be the only children there, Dad pushed Azi and me as close as possible to the demarcated line barriers so that we could get a closer look at the goings-on. This in turn meant we were dangerously close to the line of fire; the crew members were picking out passengers seemingly at random, pushing their faces into what looked like cream pies and then tossing them into the swimming pool to the great mirth of the *royal octopus*, the other crew members, and the crowd of passengers, who were cheering wildly and urging them on.

From where I was watching, I only saw the victims thrown into the pool. I did not see them re-surface. I thought they had drowned. If any of those crew members should so much as even look in my direction, I thought I would die. And one of them did. He noticed me peering through the barricades and walked up towards me. His face was painted white with black circles around his eyes and a garishly painted red mouth. Side by side, he and Zubaidah, our Cook, would have made quite a matching pair. He wore a torn-up shirt and black and white striped trousers cut into strips and frayed at the knees. I do not think I wet my pants, but I am sure I would have come close to it. I even forgot Dad was standing behind me and I was nestled safely in front of him. As the man knelt down to my height, he gave me a broad smile displaying a row of blackened teeth and one sparkling gold tooth. To my mind, this was no smile; it was the first step towards a fatal bite. I winced and drew further back into my Dad's legs. Azi seemed to be taking it all in his stride and responded by waving to the man and saying "Hello"! It appeared Azi would not have noticed if the man had walked up to him and bit him. The man then turned to me and smiled again. From behind his back, he suddenly fished out two lollipops that he held before us. "One for you, son…" he said jovially as he handed Azi the first one, "and the other for you, darling!" as he held the other one for me. Azi did not need to be invited twice. I, however, hesitated; perhaps if I stretched out my hand, he would grab it and then bite me, or worse still throw me into the pool. I then heard Dad's soothing and reassuring voice, "It's okay, Girlie, you can take it. The man is not going to harm you."

"Thank you, mister," I said, as I slowly stretched out my hand to take it, whilst observing him with the suspicion of a mouse contemplating a piece of cheese stuck in a mouse trap. I got my lollipop and as he stood up, he ruffled my hair as a gesture of affection before returning to the festive activities.

We arrived at Colombo port six days later with no further incidents of Azi persecuting me for my bunk, without any green regal octopus requiring amusement, nor any bizarre crew members with blackened teeth hovering menacingly about looking for small children!

We stayed at the Galle Face Hotel in Colombo, which is an old colonial-styled hotel at the Esplanade beside the sea. It was a stately looking building with a long flight of stairs leading to the upper floor where our rooms were located. The hotel staff seemed older than the building; I wondered how those tottering old men could carry all our luggage up the flight of stairs before noticing a cage elevator on the ground floor, operated by another old chap wearing a white uniform and a pill box hat. Our rooms were spacious but smelt a little musty. Mum reckoned that as the hotel was so close to the sea, the salty sea air billowing through the open windows caused the curtains and linen to become damp. She cautioned that we were not to go anywhere near the beach or the seaside because the waves were enormously powerful and the sea current strong. And indeed, they were. Our rooms had an unimpeded view of the sea and the waves crashing on the shoreline with a sizeable froth like a giant milkshake. In front of the hotel was a long green field in which there were groups of families enjoying their own picnics and young boys playing cricket with their makeshift wickets, markers, and bats. We stayed at the hotel for three days, during which time there appeared to be wagon loads of relatives calling upon Mum and Dad, none of whom I had ever seen or met. I have never ever understood this strange phenomenon about aunts. What is it about aunts, that they should feel it their duty and obligation to pinch the cheeks of their nieces and nephews, as a measure of endearment? Or is it out of disdain or utter madness? With Mum having eight sisters, this meant that we got our cheeks pinched eight times and, in some cases, by the uncles as well, bumping up the number of times. It is no wonder, then, that after Day One, both Azi and I disappeared with Ah Chwee and Merifa to go walkabout when we heard that the dreaded aunts would be back to see Mum.

On the fourth day in Colombo, our *ayahs* packed our belongings as they informed us that we were going to take a train to my grandfather's coconut plantation and tea estate in a place called *Nuwara Eliya*. So off we went to the Railway Station accompanied by three of Mum's unmarried sisters to take the train to the Estates. Dad had to pay for the three spinsters as well (of course), and we were all booked with sleeping berths as the train ride was an overnight journey. Azi and I together with our ayahs were in one compartment. As with the incident on the ship, Azi wanted the berth which I was allocated and as such, a squabble ensued until Mum suddenly appeared at the compartment door wielding the cane. She did not need to say anything — her wide-open eyes and her wagging the cane up and down in the air was enough to quell our disagreement. In fact, as soon as she left, we both looked at each other with a facial expression that read, "I thought *you* were supposed to hide the cane!"

We were met at the *Nuwara Eliya* Railway Station by my Mum's eldest brother, who had taken charge and quite rightly, inherited my grandfather's Estate upon his, and later, my grandmother's, deaths. As soon as the train came to a halt, a battalion of coolies came to the train doors to help passengers alight and carry the luggage. One particular coolie stood in front of me and as he reached up to try and lift me down from the train, I caught a whiff of his putrid body odour from his exposed armpits. It was a rancid smell of something decaying; like the odour of fermented soya beans, and the stench went straight up my nostrils to my sinuses. This man was evidently a stranger to a bar of soap. I simply could not dispel the smell from my senses, and this invariably gave me a headache for the entire duration of the trip to the *Nuwareliya Estate*. My Mum's elder brother, our Uncle Sunny, drove up in his Hindustan Motors Ambassador; his driver accompanied him with his second car, a Morris Minor Traveller. Despite there being two vehicles, there was still not enough room for everyone and the luggage. Mum's three sisters had to travel by trishaw to the Estate. This, of course, served to give Azi and me no end of satisfaction after having successively suffered the painful ceremonial cheek-pinching from these three aunts.

Chiltern Estate was no colonial bungalow; it was a Palladian-style mansion with fifteen bedrooms. It had, of course, suffered a little through the passage of time and two World Wars, but all in all, it was still a magnificent structure. There was a beautifully manicured garden with brilliantly coloured bougainvillaea growing rampantly at every turn of the eye. There were trees fruiting with guavas, mangoes, avocados, bananas and of course, coconuts aplenty.

Uncle Sunny had in his employment, a team of twenty workers for the coconut and the tea plantations and five for the actual residence. He lived quite comfortably there and as he appeared to have all of his living requirements easily availed to him, saw no purpose to take a wife. Unlike his younger brother, our despicable Uncle Jack, Uncle Sunny was a benevolent and jovial uncle. He was generous to a fault, and it appeared that all his staff and servants took very kindly to him. Despite not being a married man, he liked children. There were chocolates and sweets readily available, and he made sure that our *ayahs* were provided with any and all necessities required in order to keep us comfortable and content.

The following day after our arrival, Uncle Sunny whispered to Azi and me his best-kept secret. He told us there were hundreds of squirrels that ran around the residence grounds. He said that if we were to sit still in a chair on the verandahs, with a pinch of salt in the open palms of our hands, a squirrel or two would be sure to come up to our palms to nibble on the salt. Then we could catch them and could keep them as pets. And that is precisely how we spent most of our time at Chiltern Estate, sitting quietly in a chair on the verandahs, waiting for a squirrel to come over to us. Although we saw scores of squirrels running all about the garden, not a single one came to our hands during the entire week that we were there.

It was only during the trip back from S.S. *Australia* to

MY FATHER IS POLICE, LAH!

Singapore, that Dad elucidated us with the proverbial dropping penny. He said, guffawing, "That little snippet was your Uncle Sunny's brilliant ruse to keep you young children quietly entertained in his house."

Azi was particularly miffed that he had not caught on to Uncle Sunny's trickery earlier. On account of his unprecedented bout of idiocy, he had let the wily side of his character down against Uncle Sunny's superior wit. This Snake child had allowed himself to be bamboozled.

19

SHOULD AULD ACQUAINTANCE

A few weeks after we returned to Singapore and after being restored to our usual daily routines, Dad called me to him one evening, whilst he settled into his favourite evening tipple of scotch and soda and lit a cigarette. He said softly, "Girlie, in a few months' time you will get a new *ayah*."

"Why? What's wrong with *auntie* Merifa?" I asked puzzled by this sudden announcement.

"Nothing is wrong with her, Girl. It is just that the time has come for her to get married. Once she gets married, she will have to follow her husband, and then she will have children of her own to look after."

I was not particularly close to my *ayah* even though she was totally endeared to me, as evidenced by the tumultuous incident involving Uncle Jack. Ah Chwee, however, was extremely fond of Azi and also of me for that matter, but she was careful not to interfere with nor encroach upon Merifa's childminding style, as it was not her station to do so.

"Then who is going to be my *ayah*? Ah Chwee?" I asked Dad, indicating that Merifa's forthcoming marriage and exit were not going to unnecessarily traumatise me.

"Mum has found you a new *ayah* from Ceylon. Her name is

Maybelle, and she will be arriving in Singapore soon. Mum said that she is already married but has no children. I think she will love you and take care of you very well," he replied calmly, in the hope this sudden announcement was not going to unsettle me.

Merifa initially did not say anything to me about her forthcoming marriage. Whether she thought I was too young to know about such things, or simply that it was none of my business, I cannot be sure. But if it were the case of the latter, she would be wrong; it *was* my business because she was my *ayah*. Shortly before bedtime one night, as Merifa brushed my long hair, I asked her, "Auntie Merifa, are you leaving our house?"

"Yes, child. I am going to start a family of my own and you will have a new *ayah*. Are you worried?" she asked with gentleness in her voice.

"No," I replied, "I'm not worried, I'm only sad you are going away."

She hugged me tightly swaying from side to side as if she were slightly inebriated. Then she continued brushing my hair at which time I distinctly heard her sniffing slightly. I had made her cry.

For the few weeks approaching Merifa's wedding, she and Mum were busy traipsing around Arab Street and Hill Street, purchasing all the clothes and apparel she would be requiring for her trousseau. This time around, Dad left them to get on with the task themselves for fear of another 'rat episode' erupting. Daeri drove them to wherever they needed to go and each time they returned, Merifa would come back with several pairs of new shoes, handbags, colourful silk Indian *sarees* and gold jewellery. She always returned with a small trinket for me, sometimes a little key fob, or a small leather coin purse, or just simply a packet of sweets. Mum bought her sets of linen, tableware, bedding, and even gave her the extra sets of crockery, glasses, and cutlery which she did not need, probably because they were all odd or incomplete sets thanks to parties' breakages.

Unbeknownst to Azi and me, another purpose of the voyage to Ceylon was not just honouring the covenant with Azi for his bravery at his *Bersunat* Ceremony, it was also to meet with Merifa's prospective husband's family and relatives in Colombo to decide whether the match was a suitable one. Merifa had been match-made with a male cousin twice-removed, a young soldier in the British Army. It looked like history was going to repeat itself. Dad was underwriting the cost of the young soldier's return passage to Singapore and then he and his new bride would be sailing back to Ceylon to start their new life. Dad was also underwriting the costs of the wedding celebration to be held in Singapore at our house. There was going to be another massive Malay *kenduri* at our prestigious bungalow!

Zubaidah was again given the task of being the chief caterer for the wedding. Not only that, but she was also given the illustrious position of the *Mak Andam*. This position is similar in the station to that of a matron of honour but with huge responsibilities for taking charge of the bride-to-be. For example, it was a Malay custom that the *Mak Andam* would have to establish whether or not the bride was a virgin. In order to evaluate this, the *Mak Andam* would snip off a few hairs from the girl's forehead and watch how the hair falls. The manner of the hair falling would dictate the required answer. I am not sure how this all pans out and works scientifically, but this was the custom. Go figure.

The *Mak Andam* also ensures the beautifying ritual of the bride before the wedding and this long drawn-out process is carried out in the privacy of the bride's room. This could include filing the bride's teeth with a special filing stone to straighten them, and also applying the henna paste to the bride's hands and feet as a mark of beauty, trimming her eyebrows and wrapping her waist tightly in yards of cloth to reduce her waistline. Traditionally, Muslim Malay brides do not wear nail lacquer as it is believed the lacquer prevents water from touching the nails during the ablution process, prior to performing their daily prayers. Therefore henna, being nothing more than a dye, is the more favoured medium of beautification for the hands and feet. As Merifa was too busy preparing for her forthcoming wedding, Ah Chwee was given charge of me temporarily, until the new *ayah's* scheduled arrival.

And so began the groundwork for the Wedding Ceremony as was the case with Azi's *Bersunat* Ceremony. A large tent for the dining area, as well as the stage, had to be erected in the garden, with a decorative raised platform called a *pelamin* on the stage, where the bride and groom would be seated upon two thrones to receive well-wishers and relatives. Mum made a point to instruct Kebun to ensure that Zubaidah was kept beyond a radius of twenty feet, well away from the stage and platform. She did not want another demolition incident. In any case, Zubaidah had bigger fish to fry; she was the illustrious *Mak Andam* and would be the major-domo during the wedding ceremony as far as the bride was concerned. Apart from catering for the expected two hundred guests, she had to make sure that Merifa would be well prepared for marriage and a most beautiful bride. The latter part of this preparation was not going to be achievable if left to Zubaidah's own devices. As Mum already knew that Zubaidah had her own bizarre style of make-up, she commissioned a professional beautician from the Beauty Parlour at Robinsons Department Store to do Merifa's make-up on her wedding day, so that she would not look like Frankenstein's Bride, as she would if Zubaidah had anything to do with it.

As a wedding was a higher priority than a *Bersunat*, Mum instructed the servants that she wanted the entire house spruced up and spotlessly clean, especially the Master kitchen. As the cleaning commenced, even Kebun had to get in on the act to trim shrubs and bushes, tree branches thatwere hanging too low and spruce up all the flower beds and potted plants. Zubaidah, Zainal and Harris started with the master kitchen and that is when the huge commotion ensued.

I heard Zubaidah's loud shriek followed by the sound of a number of whacks with a coconut fibre broom. Then pots and pans tumbled down from their shelves onto the floor making an awful clanging noise. Mum, Rukiah, Saminah and I rushed out to the courtyard to see what the kerfuffle was about, only to see Zubaidah suddenly emerge from the kitchen with a broom in her hand, chasing a huge rodent. She called out to Kebun and Jaafar who like a two-man infantry brigade hastened to assist, with Kebun holding a *cangkul*, not dissimilar to a hoe, over his shoulder and Jaafar holding pruning clippers. As soon as Mum saw the rat, she immediately pivoted on her heels and ran indoors. This *mutant ninja* rat was huge. Not a single one amongst our contingent of cats showed even the mildest bit of interest in attacking it—and for good reason, too. The rat was larger, fiercer, and speedier than they. It was probably the *godfather* of all the other rodents that found it perfectly all right to squat in our house. As our house was a bungalow with a garden, there was no escape from both little and big critters. As long as the rodents and vermin did not enter the living quarters, Mum was fine with that. Zubaidah nonetheless was furiously in hot pursuit and with each whack of her broom, she was totally missing her target. What she lacked in marksmanship, she made up for it in enthusiasm.

Eventually, the rat was seen entering Ah Chwee's quarters. "Aaeeeyaaaaah!" Ah Chwee screamed as she darted out of her room and immediately tried to climb up onto a wooden stool.

But owing to her sudden moves and, of course, as her weight did not correspond to her height, the stool gave way. Ah Chwee's fall created a bit of a domino effect, as Zubaidah arrived on the scene followed by Kebun and Jaafar. As Ah Chwee fell she knocked Zubaidah for a six; she then fell on Kebun who landed on Jaafar. I bet the rat, who must have been watching this comedy of errors, might well have been giggling to itself "tee-hee-hee". Once they had all picked themselves off the ground and the accusations as to who was at fault had ceased, I peered into Ah Chwee's room and saw the rat's tail sticking out from behind the Kwan Yin statue. This must have been a rather pious rat and a Buddhist no less. It was seeking refuge behind Kwan Yin. I drew this to Ah Chwee's attention, and she immediately forbade Zubaidah or the other two from going anywhere into her room, let alone near her statue.

"*Ta'boleh masuk aah!...*" she commanded with a stern voice, forbidding the trio from entering her domain, "*...nanti gua sendiri tangkap ah!*" she continued, purportedly claiming that she would catch the critter by herself.

"*Apa macam lu mau tangkap? Kau gila, takut tikus ah!*" shouted Zubaidah accusingly, citing Ah Chwee's fear and trepidation of going near, let alone catching, any living intruder with more than two legs. By this time, Jaafar had arrived at the most feasible and sensible solution to the problem. He brought a rat trap cage containing a piece of dried fish as bait. This was Mum's humane form of trapping rats rather than using the snap trap variety that often left an awful mess. Once the trap was in place, Ah Chwee started to sing to the rat in Cantonese. Not only was this a Buddhist rat, but it also evidently held a Chinese passport. Perhaps it had arrived in Singapore as a refugee on a slow boat from Canton? Or travelled together with Mrs Long's luggage from Hong Kong? Absurd as the thought might have been, the rat appeared to listen to Ah Chwee's song and slowly walked into the cage, took hold of the dried fish with its two front paws and the trap door snapped shut. Ah Chwee then carried the cage, held it at arms-length, and continued to sing to the rat. In Cantonese. I expect she was reassuring the rodent that it would not be put to death but would be taken far, far, away to a place where it could join its comrades living in an environment totally conducive to rodents, a rubber or oil palm plantation across the Causeway in Malaya. Zubaidah, now feeling rather elated that this giant rodent was finally caught, asked Mum if she could take it and dispose of it somewhere far away. Mum figured that Zubaidah wanted to keep the rat and taunt it to death. Apart from anything else, Zubaidah had a poor sense of direction — not only could she not tell the difference between a road map and a hole in the ground, but she also would not have been able to find her way out of a bucket! Mum gave Daeri the task of delivering the rat to freedom, across the Causeway.

Finally, the commencement of the Wedding was upon us. The bridegroom, whom I only knew as *'Aahmed'* had arrived from Ceylon and was staying at one of his relative's homes. The house and grounds were again resplendent with colourful tents, bedecked with buntings, *bunga manggar* tinsel glittering in the sunshine, and garden oil lamps affixed onto bamboo poles symbolically illuminating the driveway to herald the arrival of the bridegroom, the *kompang* players and all other chattels and paraphernalia customary in a Malay Wedding. The family members again wore special traditional outfits embellished and adorned with accoutrements pertaining to Dad's heritage. Our effervescent *Mak Andam* Zubaidah was poised and ready to await the arrival of the bridegroom whom she would traditionally accost, playfully demanding payment from him prior to permitting him to acquire his bride.

MY FATHER IS POLICE, LAH!

The first stage of the Wedding Ceremony was the solemnisation of the Contract, known as the *Nikah,* whereupon a *Kadhi* who would be the Islamic magistrate officiating the *Nikah* procedure, would be called upon to solemnise the marriage. Alternatively, the bride's father or older brother could perform the solemnisation. As Dad was Merifa's older brother, he was tasked as a deputy to the officiating *Kadhi*. During the *Nikah* procedure, first of all Merifa was asked whether she voluntarily was entering into the marriage without duress being placed upon her, and upon her answer being agreeable, Dad spoke to Aahmed to establish his intentions. The Oath of Matrimony had to be taken from the bridegroom, whereupon he had to repeat the Oath in one breath, without pause or mistake, whilst clasping the Kadhi's hand, before the marriage Contract was signed. He managed this admirably and in one attempt, failing which, he would have to repeat the Oath again and again until he got it flawlessly right. Mum referred to him as *'the One Take Wonder'*.

Thereafter Aahmed offered a valuable gift to the bride after the solemnisation — a solid gold necklace around her neck and a gold wedding ring on her ring finger. This action also symbolises the husband's duty to his wife to fulfil her everyday requirements during the entire course of their marriage.

After the solemnisation, Aahmed and Merifa were to present themselves for the *Bersanding* Ceremony, where the bride and bridegroom sit upon the ceremonial Wedding dais on stage and are treated as a *king* and *queen* for a day. Merifa looked resplendent in her Javanese-styled traditional attire. Her hair was coiffed into a beehive style with a lavish gold tiara placed upon her head, further embellished with golden hair clasps, *cucuk sanggul* and hair beads cascading down the sides of her head. As she was Dad's youngest sister, that made her a princess. Her attire was tailored out of yellow hand-woven *kain songket* and her future husband, who was a cousin twice removed and also of a direct royal line, was given the privilege of wearing yellow as well. Merifa wore heavy gold bangles and adornments around her neck, wrists and even around her ankles. She could well have been wearing the equivalent value of a small new semi-detached house in Ceylon, around her person.

By this time, the guests and well-wishers had arrived, and the Wedding was progressing at full strength. Zubaidah had, as usual, done a splendid job with the catering and she took her place as the Mak Andam at the side of Merifa, holding a decorated fan in front of Merifa's face to symbolise the bride's demureness and virtue. The Malay women in attendance were dressed in their traditional finery and bedecked in gold ornaments, as was Zubaidah who enjoyed being part of the *Bersanding* Ceremony and taking in all the attention, which was not actually meant for her, but for the bridal couple. Had Dad not been a Police Officer with access to policemen patrolling the vicinity, our celebratory traditional events such as this, could have provided rich pickings for prospective armed robbers.

One by one the well-wishers approached the bridal couple to offer their blessings and gifts, which the *Mak Andam* acknowledged, although it was not her place to do so. But Merifa just let Zubaidah enjoy herself and feel important. When I went up to the couple, I walked straight up to Merifa and held her hand. I stood solemnly beside her, nestling myself as close as possible to her. We both instinctively knew that this was my way of saying goodbye to her. *Aahmed* leaned forward to try and take my hand in an attempt to endear himself to me, but I would not let go of Merifa's hand. In sum, I simply ignored him. Dad, Mum and Azi had followed me up to the *pelamin* and whilst Mum and Azi sprinkled the customary rose water from a silver votive flask onto the bridal couple, Dad held out his hand to me and said,

MY FATHER IS POLICE, LAH!

"Come Girlie, time to leave."

I looked up at Merifa's beautifully made-up face and stared deeply into her eyes. She looked back and was trying hard not to let any tears well up in her eyes, lest they should cause her heavy make-up to run and cause an avalanche on her face.

As I walked with Dad into the house, he looked at me and smiled. "Be happy for her," he consoled. "This is not a time to be sad, because everything in life will change. Nothing is forever. She will never forget you and I know you will not forget her."

The Wedding Ceremony lasted more than six hours and this time around, Dad had not invited his Colonial friends to the Event because he was not going to have any alcoholic drinks served at all, with the *Kadhi* being in attendance. By the time we went to bed at 8:00 p.m., the bridal couple had retired to the bridal chamber. This was one room in the servants' quarters which had been vacated for the purpose, lavishly beautified, and furnished befitting a royal couple to spend their first marital night together. I expect someone amongst the household staff was forewarned to take the necessary precautionary steps so as to ensure that no stray rodent should suddenly make an ill-timed appearance in the bridal chamber during this momentous night.

The following morning, Merifa and Aahmed had to undergo the Bridal Ceremonial Bath as the final part of the bridal ceremony. Normally this *Bersiram* ritual is carried out a week after the *Bersanding*. However, as their ship was due to sail at 5:00 p.m. that day for Colombo, the *Bersiram* had to be done that morning. The bridal couple, both dressed in ordinary simple clothing, were then seated on two individual chairs with a broad yellow cloth suspended over their heads by our Malay servants. Then several pails of water infused with limes and flowers were poured over them while Moulana chanted some prayers and gave them marital blessings. Once this final ritual was over, the new couple went away to get ready for their long journey to Ceylon. By mid-afternoon, all Merifa's trousseau and chattels were loaded into the lorry that Dad had chartered; the number of steel trunks and other luggage Mum had arranged for Merifa, could have clothed, furnished, and decorated an entire village and its inhabitants. It was obviously a tearful parting for Merifa and the other servants, who gave her small tokens of gold ornaments and jewellery as wedding presents. As there was not enough room in Dad's Austin for everyone to accompany the new couple to the Keppel docks, just Mum and Dad went with them. Merifa kneeled down to me as she said her goodbyes and she placed in my hand a small miniature book about the size of a twenty-cent coin. I looked at the book; it was a miniature Quran.

"Keep this always with you and never stray from the Perfect Word of God," she said as she kissed both my cheeks, "Never forget, you are very special to me."

With that she bade goodbye to Azi and then climbed into the car with Aahmed. As I waved goodbye, I saw Merifa looking out at me from the rear window. She kept looking at me until the car was out of sight. Zubaidah was frantically waving her hand up and down so enthusiastically that after some time, she began to feel the ache of her upper arm muscles from all the waving and resorted to supporting her waving hand with her other hand. She and Ah Chwee, being duly supported by Kebun and Jaafar respectively, each stood upon a wrought iron chair — I doubt a wooden one would have supported either of their weights — to avail them a grandstand view of the departing couple.

When you finally let go, something better will come your way. Two weeks later, Maybelle arrived in Singapore.

My new *ayah* had arrived.

Epilogue

This is a work of non-fiction, inspired by my own life experiences and recollections from when I was eight years of age. I have refused to reside within literary boundaries, and elected to reflect the realities, insanities, absurdities, ironies, comedies, and contradictions present in post-globalisation human cultures through my writing.

The incidents and characters contained herein are real, as best as I can remember them. I have changed the names of characters, some dates, people, places, and sequences to extend some privacy to those who may still be living and to the families of those who may have passed on.

Several generations have evolved, and with that several Malay and Asian customs also have been discontinued since I was eight years old. To some extent, modernisation has replaced some of the Malay traditional customs to complement newer trends in behavioural patterns and, of course, the advent of a more defined Islamic sensibility has created a situation whereby Muslim Malays are obliged to dispense with certain traditional Malay cultural customs, some of which are now regarded as *syirik*, indicating a conflict with the belief in one God.

We lived at our colonial bungalow at 409 New Bridge Road until 1970 whereupon the People's Action Party Government required the land for urban renewal. Today, the entire spread of land for the eight colonial bungalows is now occupied by a Police Complex. The kindergarten and Church buildings still remain as far as I am aware, but I believe the Church has been de-commissioned. The last time I drove past, the place was desolate and there were signposts reading, "Government Land — Trespassers will be Prosecuted" erected at all the access ways leading into the property. Perhaps this will be a landmark building preserved and restored under the National Heritage Monument Programme. Alternatively, perhaps they will be demolished for urban renewal, I do not know.

My old school has been moved to another location as the land upon which it stood has also been taken over by the Government, despite campaigns by some former students to preserve the old premises. The new school premises are nothing as individualistic and charming as the old one — another example of an aesthetic disaster when land space is of no moral concern, and affluence presents itself as a defining factor. But to be fair, the old school also stood on prime land.

MacDonald House still stands in exactly the same spot as it did when it was bombed. The Government has declared the building a Heritage Site and the Hongkong & Shanghai Banking Corporation operates its central banking facility within the building.

As for Maria Hertogh, she was ultimately removed from Singapore by the Secret Police Constabulary and reunited with her biological parents in Holland. Her original marriage to a Muslim Malay teacher in 1950 had been annulled by the then Colonial government on the grounds that she was only thirteen years, under age, at the time of the wedding. She remarried in Holland in 1955 and thereafter entered into several more marriages after divorces, until her death in 1972.

Most of our servants went their separate ways after we moved from our bungalow except for Maybelle. She became the general housekeeper, cook and lady's maid all rolled into one at our new house, a private three-storey residence within a gated compound. Azi and I had outgrown the need for ayahs. My parents, however, outsourced the services of an ethnic Chinese washer-woman and gardener, both of whom lived at a pig farm village, mercifully situated quite a distance from our new abode.

I did not hear much about the other servants nor their children after we moved, except for Jaafar, who was Kebun and Zubaidah's son. It seems he was 'trouble in trousers' going in and out of jail as if it was a cinema. I suppose how Jaafar became a recalcitrant youth in later years, should not be a surprise, having Zubaidah, an eccentric squawking mother on one side and Kebun, a meek long-suffering father on the other. What Kebun ever saw in Zubaidah was always a mystery to us, unless it was simply good entertainment value. Therein lies the speculative aspect in arranged marriages of all ethnicities.

My elder sister Yuwari, from whom I was separated at a very early age, has been an integral part of my adult life for many years. She and I have become extremely close. She still lives in Thailand, in a remote provincial town called Saraburi, in the middle of picturesque sunflower and corn fields. I watched her two sons grow into adults following our reunion 25 years after our separation, and both boys are now successful entrepreneurs living in Bangkok. Yuwari's psychic powers, through her Spiritual Masters, revisited her after she reached adulthood when the remedial effect of the Surathani Buddhist monk's ritual with the two coins waned over the years. Her abilities evolved incredibly and with alacrity. However, I resist from delving further into this aspect of my sister's life, as some regard supernatural abilities and spiritualism with a hefty dose of scepticism and contempt, not to mention sacrilege. My Dad's wisdom of "discretion being the better part of valour" springs to the fore.

Dad lived to the ripe old age of 89 and passed away on August

11, 2014, two days after Singapore's National Day. I expect he wanted to take his final salute at the Parade. He remained a loyal government servant to Prime Minister Lee Kuan Yew until his death, which preceded PM Lee's death by only seven months.

Azi passed away in January 2021, during the Covid-19 epidemic, succumbing to a barrage of life-threatening ailments which could neither be treated nor alleviated, as he was living alone in a house in Johore, Malaysia. Nobody could get to him owing to the Lockdown. As a final attempt to rescue him, a team of medical officers in Personal Protective Equipment not dissimilar to Hazmat Suits reached him. They intended to transfer him to a designated Singapore 'safe house' hotel. Azi collapsed and was rushed to the Tan Tock Seng Hospital. The medical team could not resuscitate him, and he passed away. Azi's passing, of course, inflicted exceptionally severe trauma on my mother, who survived him, in contravention of the norm of parents dying before their children. Tragically, neither she nor I could even attend his funeral owing to the Lockdown. Azi died and was buried a lonely man. Mum never overcame Azi's passing before her. I am amazed that the trauma did not severely impact her frailty as she was 101 years old. In fact, Dad's passing several years earlier did not have an impact on her as powerfully as did Azi's. Oddly, she elected not to attend Dad's funeral in 2021, leaving Azi and myself to bury our father, her husband.

She lived to be 104 years old and passed away on Boxing Day, 2023. I was there beside her when she breathed her last. I buried her.

The in-between years from childhood to our teen years will be captured in the autobiographical novel, which succeeds this one. Another describes our adult years. So much water has passed under the proverbial bridge...

Very little of the old Singapore remains today as most of the old sites have been demolished due to urban renewal. The quaint and individualistic landmark sites of the famous Orchard Road in the 1960s have all made way for futuristic concrete structures emulating just another downtown big city, except for the luscious trees on both sides of the road. I suppose that is just one of the sacrifices that had to be made for Singapore to progress from a developing to a developed country.

The post-colonial Singapore Government has struck an exceptionally fine balance — giving Singaporeans a better, cleaner, safer, and more harmonious place to inhabit by eliminating racial discord, significantly minimising, if not completely eradicating, corruption and illegal activities, and governing with a strict but fair and prudent style of administration.

Although my parents' ancestors were forced to forfeit their regnal titles, constitutional domain, imperial legacy, wealth and majestic power when they were banished from their sultanates and exiled to Ceylon by the Dutch colonials, notwithstanding this abject humiliation and disgrace, their royal heritage could not be ignored. It manifests itself in their breeding.

I consider myself extremely fortunate that my father made that life-changing decision to immigrate to Singapore when he did, liberated from the (then) insular parameters of the Ceylon Malay community, settled down in Singapore with a wife of similar heritage, produced a family and ultimately became a full-fledged Singapore citizen.

Whatever is said and done, their royal blood runs in my veins.

Acknowledgements

This autobiographical effort was the brainchild of my elder sister Yuwari, who asked me to share a part of the family's life and experiences, get it down on paper and out into the world. Without her encouragement and, more importantly, perseverance in egging me on to write, this book would never have materialised. Further, it would not have otherwise served as a platform to pay tribute to my parents through these quirky stories.

I also want to acknowledge the encouragement of my long-time partner — my best friend, husband and harshest critic. Thank you, RAJ, for your patience, brutal honesty, and determination to see this journey through with me.

To my tireless Editor Victoria Graham and Publisher Graham Earnshaw, thank you for your vision, patience and guidance. To my very talented and creative Designer, Tash Galasyuk, your outpour of image and design ideas and visuals is hard to beat.

My grateful thanks also to my critics, Y.M. Tunku Dato' Seri (Dr) Iskandar bin Tunku Abdullah, Malaysia; Y.M. Prof. Tunku Dr. Sara Tunku Ahmad Yahaya, Malaysia; David G. Williams, UK; Lillian Wells-Lorentzen, USA; Boon Choy Wong, Malaysia; Rosnah Ismail, Singapore; Venkiteswaran Sankar, Malaysia; Blenda Andrade, Canada and Philip M. Hawkins, Philippines and of course my classmates, Sim Suh-ting, Annie Shirwaiker, Jean Lee and others, thank you for your encouraging reviews and endorsements.

About The Author

Rowena Hawkins was born in the Year of the Monkey to privileged parents, both of whom were direct descendants of Sultans exiled to Ceylon (now Sri Lanka) from the (then) Dutch-colonised Batawie (Batavia) and Mataram (Sumatra). Both parents were, therefore, born in Ceylon in the insular Ceylon-Malay community, and not of the indigenous Singhalese ethnic inhabitants already there .

Both her parents emigrated from Ceylon to Singapore, where she was born — her father first in 1948 as a British Military Officer based originally in Ceylon and thereafter seconded to post-war Singapore, and her mother later in 1950 after marrying her father.

She was educated mostly in Singapore at two prestigious private schools. Her youth was spent pursuing a modelling career, becoming Miss Singapore in the 1970s and representing Singapore in a prestigious international beauty pageant. Then, moving across to the opposite end of a glamourous professional spectrum, being engaged by the Malaysian Red Cross Society

MY FATHER IS POLICE, LAH!

and the UNHCR to resettle 14,000 Indo-Chinese Refugees accommodated on an uninhabited island eighteen nautical miles off the East Coast of Terengganu in Malaysia, where the rat population outnumbered the human population and where one contracted dysentery as often as one caught fish for supper.

Following the two years of hardship living within the UNHCR Resettlement Programme, she moved on to Hong Kong. There, she obtained an MBA in 1998, majoring in Corporate Law and Industrial Psychology, with a lesser Discipline in International Marketing. She also worked for a British PLC and simultaneously studied for her university degrees. She honed her writing skills by producing her dissertations in English. She lived, studied, and worked in colonial Hong Kong from 1986 through to the post-colonial HKSAR in 2016.

She is now retired and is duly occupied with her menagerie; a platoon of seven rescued dogs, land turtles, aquarium fish and a host of wild critters who reside in her garden rent-free, citing 'Squatters Rights'.

www.ingramcontent.com/pod-product-compliance
Lightning Source LLC
LaVergne TN
LVHW030320070526
838199LV00069B/6511